T0071962

Healthy and Hearty
SALADS

Substantial Main Courses for Every Season

Caroline Hofberg

Photography by **Tia Borgsmidt**

Translation by **Nicholas Portice**

Skyhorse Publishing

Copyright © 2012, 2022 by Caroline Hofberg and Norstedts, Stockholm
English translation © 2014, 2022 by Skyhorse Publishing
Photography by Tia Borgsmidt
Graphic design by Ove Lindfors
First published by Norstedts, Sweden in 2012 as *Matiga sallader* by Caroline Hofberg.
Published by agreement with Norstedts Agency.
Previously published under the title *Substantial Salads*.

Skyhorse Publishing books may be purchased in bulk at special discounts for sales promotion, corporate gifts, fund-raising, or educational purposes. Special editions can also be created to specifications. For details, contact the Special Sales Department, Skyhorse Publishing, 307 West 36th Street, 11th Floor, New York, NY 10018 or info@skyhorsepublishing.com.

Skyhorse® and Skyhorse Publishing® are registered trademarks of Skyhorse Publishing, Inc.®, a Delaware corporation.

www.skyhorsepublishing.com

10 9 8 7 6 5 4 3 2 1

Library of Congress Cataloging-in-Publication Data is available on file.

ISBN: 978-1-5107-6486-6
Ebook ISBN: 978-1-5107-7014-0

Cover design by David Ter-Avanesyan
Cover photo credit: Tia Borgsmidt

Printed in China

Contents

Introduction

AS ALWAYS, IT'S ALL ABOUT THE QUALITY OF THE INGREDIENTS. The preparation doesn't have to be complicated or time-consuming. On the contrary, if you use high quality raw ingredients, you shouldn't hide a thing with fancy tricks. Of course, one must consider what the season has to offer. We have a truly unique environment and wonderful seasons that cause us to lead different "food lives" in the spring/summer than in the autumn/winter. Seasons are, in a way, nature's own way of inspiring us, especially in our cooking.

During the darkest days of the year, dishes become a little heavier and more robust. When the temperature falls to below freezing, it's probably not a cool salad you're longing for. But the alternative doesn't have to be slow-cooking and thick stews. It's entirely possible to warm yourself up with a substantial salad that contains the season's nutritious and flavorful raw ingredients. During this time of year, we should walk right past the produce section with its tomatoes, cucumbers, and iceberg lettuce. These taste best in the summer and besides a salad can be so much more than a simple house salad with tomatoes and cucumbers.

During the autumn and winter, we should be sure to enjoy root vegetables and mushrooms. And the cabbage! Why is it so easy to forget about all the wonderful types of cabbage? With exciting grains, pastas, lentils, and beans we can make rustic, warm, and hearty salads—precisely the type of food you'd like to have these times of the year.

So little by little, the light and the warmth return. Now, lazy summer days, sunshine and sunbathing should be your only concern. And truth be told, the summer activities and the hammocks are a lot more enticing than standing in the kitchen cooking. Ideally, summer food should be easy to make. The summer really invites a simple, everyday luxury. The grill comes out, fresh berries are enjoyed directly from the bushes. Sun-ripened fruit and sumptuous vegetables are wonderful gifts in the summer kitchen that are perfect when combined in a delightful salad.

Trying to choose one season over another is simply impossible. They are all wonderful and all represent the joy of cooking in their own way. Be inspired, take stock of the season's magnificent raw ingredients and make delicious and substantial salads all year round!

Bulgur Wheat with Chanterelles and Lingonberries

This warm bulgur salad with chanterelles, lingonberries, and goat cheese exudes autumn. This salad is excellent as an entrée; however, it is also a good accompaniment to game, lamb, or grilled salmon. The lingonberries can be substituted with dried cranberries or pomegranate seeds.

4 portions

1¼ cups (300 ml) bulgur
2½ cups (600 ml) water
1 vegetable bouillon cube
4¼ cups (1 liter) fresh chanterelles
3 shallots
butter for frying
sea salt flakes
freshly ground pepper
¾ cup (200 ml) chopped parsley
¼ cup (50 ml) fresh thyme (stems removed)
½ cup (100 ml) coarsely chopped walnuts
⅔ cup (150 ml) thawed lingonberries
7 ounces (200 g) goat cheese (chèvre)

1. Cook the bulgur according to the directions on the packaging, with the bouillon cube. Keep the bulgur warm.

2. Clean the chanterelles, and slice the larger mushrooms into smaller pieces. Peel and chop the shallots.

3. Fry the mushrooms and shallots in butter until the liquid has been absorbed.

4. Mix together the bulgur, chanterelles, parsley, thyme, walnuts, and lingonberries. Crumble the goat cheese on top and add salt and pepper to taste.

Goat Cheese Salad with Berries and Candied Nuts

This fresh salad with berries, goat cheese, and candied nuts is a superb summer meal. Here, I serve it with thinly sliced Parma ham, but it's also a home run with grilled lamb.

4 portions

approx. 3½ cups (800 ml) of berries such as blueberries, raspberries, and strawberries
14 ounces (400 g) wheat berries
3½ ounces (100 g) tender salad greens such as red chard, arugula, spinach
7 ounces (200 g) goat cheese (chèvre)
3 tablespoons olive oil
2 tablespoons aged balsamic vinegar or crema di balsamico
sea salt flakes
freshly ground pepper
¼–½ pound (150–200 g) Parma ham (Prosciutto di Parma), thinly sliced

Candied Nuts
1 deseeded and chopped chili pepper
3½ ounces (100 g) pecans
2 tablespoons honey
2 tablespoons raw sugar
¼ teaspoon cinnamon
a pinch of cayenne pepper

1. **Begin with the Nuts:** Preheat the oven to 425°F (225°C). Combine all ingredients for the candied nuts on a baking sheet lined with parchment paper.

2. Roast in the middle of the oven for approximately 6 minutes. Remove from oven and fold together so the nuts mix well with the sugar. Let the nuts chill, and break into smaller pieces.

3. **The Salad:** Rinse the berries and halve the larger strawberries. Rinse and drain the wheat berries.

4. Plate the greens first, then the wheat berries and other berries, and crumble cheese on top. Drizzle with olive oil and balsamic vinegar. Add salt and pepper to taste.

5. Sprinkle the candied nuts on and garnish with ham when ready to serve.

Chicken Salad with Tuna Sauce

A substantial and summery salad that is a successful combination of Salad Niçoise and Vitello Tonnato. Paired with this flavorful dressing, this salad is a favorite in my summer kitchen.

4 portions

5 ounces (150 g) haricots verts (or green beans)
1 can large white beans (14 ounces/400 g)
1 grilled chicken
½ cucumber
9 ounces (250 g) cherry tomatoes
3 tablespoons olive oil
2 tablespoons freshly squeezed lemon juice
sea salt flakes
freshly ground pepper
1 head romaine lettuce
4 hardboiled eggs
2 scallions
½ cup (100 ml) black olives

Dressing
1 can of tuna fish in water
2 tablespoons capers
3 tablespoons mayonnaise
2 tablespoons freshly squeezed lemon juice
⅓ cup (75 ml) sour cream
sea salt flakes
freshly ground pepper

1. Cook the green beans in lightly salted water until soft. Let cool. Rinse the white beans and drain.

2. Split the chicken into smaller pieces. Cut the cucumber into pieces, and halve the tomatoes.

3. Mix together the beans, chicken, cucumber, tomatoes, olive oil, and lemon juice. Add salt and pepper to taste.

4. Arrange the lettuce on a serving plate. Divide the chicken salad evenly. Top with egg wedges, thinly sliced scallions, and olives. Serve with the dressing.

5. **The Dressing:** Drain the tuna fish. Mix the ingredients and add salt and pepper to taste.

Beet Salad with Bacon and Bleu Cheese

The saltiness from the bleu cheese and bacon is a great complement to the beet's natural sweetness. The lentils are delicious and nutritious and make for a hearty meal.

4 portions

1 pound (500 g) beets
1 can lentils (14 ounces/400 g)
5 ounces (140 g) bacon
2 pears
approx. 3⅓ cups (800 ml) frisée lettuce
3 tablespoons olive oil
2 tablespoons aged balsamic vinegar or
     crema di balsamico
sea salt flakes
freshly ground pepper
5 ounces (140 g) bleu cheese
2 ounces (50 g) walnuts

1. Cook the beets in lightly salted water until tender. The length of time depends on the size of the beets. Leave the root ends and a portion of the stem in, as this holds in the color and the beets will taste better.

2. Rinse the beets under cold water, pulling away the skin while they are still warm, and cut into wedges.

3. Drain the lentils. Fry the bacon until crispy and let dry on paper towels. Cut the pears into wedges.

4. Arrange the lettuce, lentils, and beets on plates. Drizzle oil and vinegar on top. Sprinkle with crumbled cheese, chopped nuts and bacon. Add pepper to taste.

Pesto Beans with Mortadella

Summer meals shouldn't be complicated. A salad is perfect to mix together, even in a simple vacation home kitchen. Moreover, this fresh Italian summer salad doesn't even need a stove!

4 portions

2 cans large white beans (each 14 ounces/400 g)
1 can artichoke hearts (14 ounces/400 g)
½ cup (100 ml) pesto, homemade or store-bought
sea salt flakes
freshly ground pepper
2 ounces (50 g) arugula
approx. 1½ pounds (700 g) melon such as ogen melon
    or cantaloupe
½ cup (100 ml) black olives
approx. 7 ounces (200 g) sliced mortadella

Pesto (¾ cup/200 ml)
½ cup (100 ml) pine nuts
1 garlic clove, chopped
1 bunch fresh basil
½ cup (100 ml) freshly grated Parmesan
½ cup (100 ml) olive oil
sea salt flakes
freshly ground pepper

1. **Begin with the Pesto:** Blend together nuts, garlic, and basil. Add in the cheese and lastly the olive oil. Add salt and pepper to taste.

2. **The Salad:** Rinse beans and let drain. Drain artichoke hearts, and halve them.

3. Combine the beans and artichoke hearts with the pesto and add salt and pepper to taste. Add half of the arugula to the artichoke salad just before serving.

4. Cut the melon into wedges and remove the seeds.

5. Arrange the artichoke and arugula salad on plates and sprinkle with olives and mortadella. Top with the remaining arugula.

Bulgur-Stuffed Eggplant with Tzatziki

Eggplant salad in a "bowl." A wonderfully spiced bulgur salad with feta cheese and mint is a perfect filling for the relatively neutral flavor of eggplant. I serve this as an entrée with tzatziki, but these eggplants are also a good complement to grilled lamb and tomato salad. A delightful variation is to flavor the tzatziki with freshly chopped mint.

4 portions

Stuffed Eggplants
4 eggplants
olive oil for brushing
sea salt flakes
¾ cup (200 ml) bulgur
1¾ cups (400 ml) water
1 vegetable bouillon cube
1 red onion
2 garlic cloves
2 tomatoes
3 tablespoons chopped mint
½ teaspoon Sambal Oelek
7 ounces (200 g) crumbled feta

Tzatziki
½ cucumber
sea salt flakes
¾ cup (200 ml) Greek yogurt
1 garlic clove, pressed
½ tablespoon olive oil

1. **Begin with the Tzatziki:** Grate the cucumber on the roughest side of a cheese grater. Lay the cucumber in a strainer, sprinkle a little salt on top, and let drain for about 20 minutes. Press out all the liquid. Combine the cucumber, yogurt, garlic, and olive oil. Add salt to taste.

2. **The Eggplant:** Preheat the oven to 425°F (225°C). Split the eggplants lengthwise, brush with olive oil and lightly salt. Lay them out on a cookie sheet lined with parchment paper, and bake in the middle of the oven for about 20 minutes. Let the eggplants cool a bit, and then carefully hollow them out so the shell remains intact. Chop the eggplant flesh.

3. Boil the bulgur in bouillon, keeping it covered for about for 10 minutes. Let the steam release.

4. Finely chop the garlic and onions. Halve the tomatoes, scrape out the seeds, and cut the tomatoes into small cubes. Blend together all of the ingredients for the bulgur salad and add salt to taste.

5. Stuff the eggplants with the bulgur salad. Bake them in the middle of the oven for 10 to 15 minutes. Serve together with tzatziki.

Grilled Asparagus with Mozzarella

This is without a doubt a perfect fresh lunch salad for early summer. Grilled asparagus, mozzarella, and a flavorful dressing made from capers and sardines. Air dried ham or smoked turkey breast are a good addition for those who don't want a vegetarian salad.

4 portions

1 pound (500 g) tender green asparagus
olive oil
2 fresh mozzarella balls
approx. 2 ounces (50 g) arugula

Croutons
2–3 slices whole grain bread
olive oil
sea salt flakes

Dressing
½ cup (100 ml) chopped fresh parsley
½ cup (100 ml) olive oil
2 anchovies
2 tablespoons capers
1½ tablespoons freshly squeezed lemon juice
freshly ground pepper

1. **The Dressing:** Mix together the ingredients and add pepper to taste.

2. **The Croutons:** Preheat the oven to 425°F (225°C). Remove the crust and cut into cubes. Mix the bread, oil, and salt on a baking sheet lined with parchment paper. Roast in the middle of the oven until the bread turns color, about 5 minutes.

3. **The Salad:** Remove the lower, rougher portion of the asparagus stalks. Brush the asparagus with olive oil and cook in a grill pan or over charcoal until tender.

4. Break the cheese into smaller pieces. Arrange arugula, asparagus, and cheese on plates. Drizzle with the dressing and top with croutons.

Roasted Asparagus with Bacon

For many people, asparagus is the premier vegetable of the spring, so it's a natural choice for this Italian-inspired presummer salad. The bacon gives the asparagus a wonderful salty and smoky flavor.

4 portions

1 pound (500 g) green asparagus
5 ounces (140 g) bacon
3 tablespoons olive oil
1 tablespoon balsamic vinegar
2 teaspoons honey
sea salt flakes
freshly ground pepper
2 cans large white beans (each 14 ounces/400 g)
4 tomatoes
1 bunch of basil
¾ cup (200 ml) roughly grated Parmesan
3½ tablespoons (50 ml) roasted pine nuts

1. Preheat the oven to 425°F (225°C). Remove the lower, rougher portion of the asparagus stalks. Wrap a piece of bacon around each asparagus stalk.

2. Lay the asparagus on a cookie sheet lined with parchment paper. Roast in the middle of the oven for about 12 minutes.

3. Combine the oil, vinegar, honey, salt, and pepper.

4. Rinse the beans and let drain. Cut the tomatoes into smaller pieces. Mix together the beans, tomatoes, dressing, and basil leaves.

5. Plate the salad and top with asparagus, cheese, and nuts.

Shrimp Salad with Thousand Island Dressing

A rather filling lunch salad, for which peeling the shrimp is worth the trouble. Add a classic Thousand Island dressing and a nice bread to accompany it, and you have a really luxurious lunch!

4 portions

2¼ pounds (1 kg) unpeeled cooked shrimp
½ cucumber
1 red onion
2 avocadoes
1½ tablespoons freshly squeezed lemon juice
sea salt flakes
freshly ground white pepper
approx. 3 ounces (80 g) mixed salad greens
dill and lemon for serving

Thousand Island Dressing
1¼ cups (300 ml) sour cream
4 tablespoons Heinz chili sauce
approx. 5 dashes Tabasco
sea salt flakes

1. Begin by combining the ingredients for the dressing.

2. Peel the shrimp.

3. Cut the cucumber into pieces. Remove the onion skin and cut the onion into thin slices. Cut the avocadoes in half and remove the pits. Remove the avocado flesh with a spoon.

4. Toss together the cucumber, onion, avocado, lemon juice, salt, and pepper.

5. Divide the salad greens onto plates. Lay the vegetables on top, followed by the shrimp and dill. Serve with lemon wedges and dressing.

Beef Tenderloin with Salad Tartar

A substantial and "everyday luxury" salad with beef tenderloin.

4 portions

1–1¼ pounds (500–600 g) beef tenderloin
butter
sea salt flakes
freshly ground pepper

Salad
¾ cup (200 ml) light crème fraîche or sour cream
2 teaspoons Dijon mustard
sea salt flakes
freshly ground pepper
1 red onion
10–12 gherkins
2 heads of romaine lettuce
3 tablespoons capers
approx. 5 ounces (150 g) bleu cheese

1. Preheat the oven to 350°F (175°C). Brown the meat in butter. Add salt and pepper to taste. Afterward, cook in the oven until it reaches an internal temperature of 130°F (55°C). Cover with foil and let rest 5 to 10 minutes.

2. Combine crème fraîche and mustard. Add salt and pepper to taste. Peel and cut the onion into thin slices. Split the gherkins in half lengthwise.

3. Layer the lettuce, onion, gherkins, and capers in a large bowl. Toss with the dressing and top with crumbled bleu cheese.

4. Cut the beef tenderloin into thin slices and serve with the salad.

Spring Vegetable Salad with Smoked Turkey Breast

Here I blend new potatoes and other spring vegetables with a summery dressing made from dill mustard sauce, sour cream, and fresh herbs. Smoked turkey breast is a great addition, as is ham or smoked salmon.

4 portions

1 pound (500 g) new potatoes
3½ ounces (100 g) radishes
3½ ounces (100 g) sugar snap peas
1 small red onion

Herb Dressing
⅔ cup (150 ml) sour cream
2 tablespoons dill mustard sauce
3 tablespoons chopped dill
3 tablespoons chopped chives
sea salt flakes
freshly ground white pepper

For Serving
approx. ½ pound (200 g) thinly sliced smoked turkey breast

1. Rinse and scrub the potatoes clean. Cook them in lightly salted water until tender. Let them cool and split them in half.

2. Combine the ingredients for the dressing.

3. Cut the radishes into wedges, slice the sugar snap peas, and chop the onion. Toss the potatoes, vegetables, and the dressing. Add salt and pepper to taste.

4. Arrange the salad on plates and serve with smoked turkey breast.

Warm Root Vegetable Salad with Ham and Gorgonzola Cream

As the dark days of the year approach, it feels completely in keeping to cook with rustic root vegetables. This root vegetable salad with ham, pears, and gorgonzola cream is an excellent dish during fall and winter.

4 portions

2¼ pounds (1 kg) rutabaga, carrots, parsnips, celeriac, and beets
2 red onions
¼ cup (50 ml) olive oil
1 tablespoon rosemary
sea salt flakes
freshly ground pepper
1 can of lentils (14 ounces/400 g)
10½ ounces (300 g) smoked ham
2 pears
3½ ounces (100 g) mixed greens
2 tablespoons freshly squeezed lemon juice
½ cup (100 ml) roasted pumpkin seeds or walnuts

Gorgonzola Cream
7 ounces (200 g) gorgonzola
9 ounces (250 g) quark or cottage cheese

1. Begin by mixing together the ingredients for the gorgonzola cream.

2. Preheat the 425°F (225°C). Brush the root vegetables clean, peel the celeriac and rutabaga. Cut into small pieces. Peel and cut onions into wedges. Lay everything out on a baking sheet lined with parchment paper, placingthe beets separate so they don't stain the other vegetables. Mix with half of the oil, rosemary, salt, and pepper.

3. Roast the root vegetables in the middle of the oven until tender, 25 to 30 minutes. Stir occasionally.

4. Rinse the lentils and let them drain. Slice the ham thinly andcut the pears into wedges.

5. Mix together the root vegetables, lentils, ham, pears, mixed greens, lemon juice, and the rest of the oil. Add salt and pepper to taste. Garnish with pumpkin seeds or walnuts, and serve with the gorgonzola cream.

Mushroom Couscous with Venison and Sharp Cheddar Cream

Mushroom and smoked venison—can it get more autumnal than that? A dressing made of sharp cheddar cheese and pear or apple completes that fall feeling.

4 portions

approx. ½ pound (200 g) fresh mushrooms
1 squash
2 red onions
2 garlic cloves
canola oil for frying
¼ cup (50 ml) fresh thyme (with stems removed)
sea salt flakes
freshly ground pepper
1⅔ cups (400 ml) water
1 vegetable bouillon cube
1⅔ cups (400 ml) couscous
1 tablespoon freshly squeezed lemon juice
approx. ½ pound (200 g) thinly sliced smoked venison

Sharp Cheddar Cream
3½ ounces (100 g) finely grated cheddar cheese
¾ cup (200 ml) Greek yogurt
¾ cup (200 ml) finely cubed pear or apple
sea salt flakes
freshly ground pepper

1. Begin by combining the ingredients for the cheese cream.

2. Cut the mushrooms into smaller pieces, cut the squash into small cubes, chop the red onions and garlic. Fry the vegetables in oil in a frying pan. Mix in the thyme, add salt and pepper to taste.

3. Boil the water and bouillon. Remove from heat and stir in couscous. Cover and let stand about 5 minutes.

4. Fluff the couscous with a fork. Stir in vegetables and lemon juice. Serve the couscous with the venison and cheese cream.

Tomato Couscous with Feta

Here I cook the couscous in tomato juice, both for color and flavor. The premarinated feta cheese is perfect for use in salads, but normal feta also works well. Raisins, olives, and basil are delightful with the feta.

4 portions

1⅔ cups (400 ml) tomato juice
2 tablespoons vegetable stock
2 garlic cloves, pressed
¼ teaspoon Tabasco
⅓ cup (75 ml) raisins
1¼ cups (300 ml) couscous
2 tablespoons olive oil from marinated feta
5 ounces (150 g) cherry tomatoes, yellow if possible
1 red onion
10½ ounces (300 g) marinated feta cheese
½ cup (100 ml) black olives
1 bunch basil

1. Boil tomato juice, stock, garlic, Tabasco, and raisins in a pot.

2. Remove from heat and mix in the couscous. Cover and let the couscous absorb the liquid for about 5 minutes. Add olive oil and fluff with a fork.

3. Halve the tomatoes and chop the onion.

4. Fold the tomatoes, cheese, onion, olives, and basil leaves into the couscous.

Roast Beef and Bean Salad with Coarse Tapenade

When I buy roast beef at the deli I always ask to have it cut extra thin, so it feels juicier. Tapenade—the classical Provencal olive mixture—is supposed to be a blended puree. However, it looks more beautiful when it is chopped by hand, and you get a little more to bite into. The flavorful olive mixture is also good to mix with diced potatoes or pasta.

4 portions

approx. ½ pound (200 g) extra thinly sliced roast beef from the deli counter

Salad
1 red onion
1 yellow pepper
1 fennel bulb
1 squash
2 tablespoons olive oil
sea salt flakes
1 can large white beans (14 ounces/400 g)
5 ounces (150 g) cherry tomatoes

Tapenade
⅔ cup (150 ml) pitted black olives
2 garlic cloves
3 anchovy fillets
2 tablespoons capers
1 tablespoon fresh thyme
½ lemon, juice
2 tablespoons olive oil
freshly ground pepper

1. **Begin with the Tapenade:** Chop olives, garlic, anchovies, capers, and thyme. Mix in lemon juice, olive oil, and pepper.

2. Preheat the oven to 425°F (225°C). Peel the onion and cut into large wedges. Chop the pepper, fennel, and squash into smaller pieces. Lay the vegetables on a baking sheet lined with parchment paper. Drizzle with olive oil and add salt to taste.

3. Roast the vegetables in the middle of the oven for 20 to 25 minutes. Stir occasionally. Let cool.

4. Rinse the beans and let drain. Cut the tomatoes into halves.

5. Toss together the roasted vegetables, beans, tomatoes, and tapenade. Serve with the roast beef.

Greek Salad with New Potatoes

Greek salad is a classic. With new potatoes added, it becomes quite hearty.

4 portions

1¾ pounds (800 g) new potatoes
3 tablespoons olive oil
½ lemon, zest and juice
sea salt flakes
freshly ground pepper
1 red onion
7 ounces (200 g) cherry tomatoes
7 ounces (200 g) feta cheese
½ cup (100 ml) black olives
½ cup (100 ml) fresh oregano,
    with the stems removed

1. Rinse and scrub the potatoes clean. Cook until tender in lightly salted water and let the steam release. Halve any larger potatoes.

2. Mix the potatoes with olive oil, lemon zest and juice, salt, and pepper.

3. Peel and thinly slice the onion. Halve the tomatoes, and break the cheese into chunks.

4. Fold onions, olives, oregano into the salad. Lastly, fold in the tomatoes and cheese.

Chicken Salad with Fruit and Herb Mayonnaise

Boiled chicken thigh with creamy dressing, sun-ripened melon, and fresh figs makes for a wonderful summer salad. If you want an even more filling meal, serve with freshly cooked new potatoes.

4 portions

1¼ pounds (600 g) chicken thigh fillets
2 cups (500 ml) water
1 tablespoon chicken stock
3 tablespoons pine nuts
1 bunch Boston lettuce
sea salt flakes
freshly ground pepper
½ small melon such as ogen melon or cantaloupe
3 fresh figs

Herb Mayonnaise
3 egg yolks
1 tablespoon freshly squeezed lemon juice
1 tablespoon Dijon mustard
2 garlic cloves, chopped
2 anchovy fillets
2 tablespoons of each of the following chopped herbs: mint, basil, parsley
⅔ cup (150 ml) canola oil
freshly ground pepper

1. **Begin with the Mayonnaise:** Mix all ingredients except for the oil and pepper together with an immersion blender. Drizzle in the oil slowly while mixing. Add pepper to taste, and then let the flavor develop for about an hour.

2. **The Salad:** Trim the chicken. Boil the water and stock. Simmer the chicken in the stock, covered, for about 5 minutes. Remove the chicken and let cool.

3. Roast the nuts in a dry pan.

4. Distribute the lettuce on one large serving plate. Cut the chicken into smaller pieces and layer them on top of the salad. Add salt and pepper to taste.

5. Cut the melon and the figs into wedges.

6. Distribute the mayonnaise over the chicken, lay the fruit on top, and garnish with pine nuts.

Salmon Bulgur with Lime Yogurt

A superb everyday meal. This fresh bulgur salad with salmon and fresh lime dressing is quick and hassle-free to make.

4 portions

1¼ cups (300 ml) bulgur
2½ cups (600 ml) water
1 vegetable bouillon cube
1 mango
2 avocadoes
⅓ cup (75 ml) chopped
    cilantro
sea salt flakes
freshly ground pepper
1¼ pounds (600 g) salmon fillet
butter for frying
3 tablespoons sweet chili sauce

Lime Yogurt
¾ cup (200 ml) Greek yogurt
1 lime, zest
1–2 teaspoons honey
sea salt flakes

1. Begin by mixing together the ingredients for the lime yogurt.

2. Boil the bulgur with bouillon, covered, for about 10 minutes. Keep the bulgur warm.

3. Halve the avocadoes and mango, remove the pits, and cut into cubes.

4. Mix together the bulgur, mango, avocado, and cilantro, and add salt and pepper to taste.

5. Cut the salmon into cubes. Fry them quickly with butter in a frying pan. Add salt to taste, and blend in sweet chili sauce.

6. Add the salmon cubes to the salad and serve with lime yogurt.

Warm Apple Salad with Turkey

Roasting vegetables in the oven produces a favorite delicacy for many. However, fruit is also incredibly tasty and feels more "finished" when baked in the oven. Aside from roasted vegetables and apples, this wonderful salad contains roast turkey, whole oat groats, bleu cheese, and nuts. The turkey breast can also be substituted with chicken breast.

4 portions

2 red apples
2 red onions
1 squash
olive oil
sea salt flakes
3 ounces (75 g) walnuts
¾ cup (200 ml) whole oat groats or wheat berries
1¾ cups (400 ml) water
1 chicken bouillon cube
2 tablespoons crema di balsamico, raspberry, if available
¾ pound (400 g) turkey breast
freshly ground pepper
2 ounces (50 g) red chard or baby spinach
5 ounces (150 g) bleu cheese

1. Preheat the oven to 425°F (225°C). Cut the apples and onions in wedges. Cut the squash into thick chunks. Lay it all out on a baking sheet lined with parchment paper. Mix together with 2 tablespoons of olive oil and salt.

2. Roast in the middle of the oven for about 20 minutes. Add the nuts evenly over the mixture when there are 10 minutes of cooking time remaining. Cover with aluminum foil to keep it warm.

3. Boil the whole groats in bouillon according to the packaging instructions, for about 12 minutes. Pour out any excess bouillon and let the steam settle. Blend the groats with crema di balsamico and 2 tablespoons olive oil.

4. Cut the turkey breast into large cubes. Fry in olive oil, add salt and pepper to taste. Cover the turkey with foil to keep it warm.

5. Mix together the groats, roasted vegetables, turkey, and chard. Add salt and pepper to taste. Top with crumbled bleu cheese.

Warm Pasta Salad with Bleu Cheese

Does it feel like you're always cooking the same old meals? Here's a simple new recipe—this pasta salad actually doesn't take longer to prepare than the pasta itself.

4 portions

9 ounces (250 g) fresh broccoli
14 ounces (400 g) penne pasta
3 tablespoons olive oil
2 tablespoons freshly squeezed
    lemon juice
3½ ounces (100 g) roughly
    chopped walnuts

¼ cup (50 ml) chopped chives
3½ ounces (100 g) arugula
3½ ounces (150 g) crumbled bleu
    cheese
sea salt flakes
freshly ground pepper

1. Divide the broccoli into florets and chop the stems into thin slices.

2. Cook the pasta according to the instructions on the packaging. Add the broccoli and let cook together for about 5 minutes. Drain the water.

3. Mix the pasta and broccoli with the rest of the ingredients and add salt and pepper to taste.

Rosemary-Fried Chicken Liver with Bean Salad

Chicken liver with cream sauce and lingonberries always tastes exceptional. But the addition of a Mediterranean-inspired bean salad with fried chicken liver, garlic, and fresh rosemary adds a bit of flair.

4 portions

2 cans large white beans (each 14 ounces/400 g)
3 tablespoons olive oil
½ cup (100 ml) chopped fresh parsley
½ lemon, zest and juice
sea salt flakes
freshly ground pepper
7 ounces (200 g) cherry tomatoes
½ cup (100 ml) sun-dried tomatoes in oil
3 scallions
1 pound (500 g) chicken liver
butter for frying
3 garlic cloves, chopped
2 tablespoons chopped fresh rosemary
3½ ounces (100 g) frisée or radicchio lettuce

1. Rinse the beans and let drain. Mix with olive oil, parsley, lemon zest and juice. Add salt and pepper to taste.

2. Halve the fresh tomatoes, cut the dried tomatoes into smaller pieces, and cut the scallions into thin strips. Fold the tomatoes and scallions into the beans just before serving.

3. Trim the liver, and cut into reasonably large pieces. Fry the chicken liver quickly in butter together with the garlic and rosemary until the insides are pink. Add salt and pepper to taste.

4. Arrange the lettuce and beans on plates and distribute the fried chicken liver on top.

Pickled Herring Salad with Beets and Browned Butter

Herring and new potatoes—this is a wonderful lunch for when guests come to visit. Crispbread, aged cheese, and a glass of beer are perfect accompaniments.

4 portions

14 ounces (400 g) pickled herring fillets
8 boiled potatoes
6 small, boiled beets
approx. 2 ounces (50 g) mixed greens
3½ tablespoons (50 g) butter
½ cup (100 ml) chopped chives

Dressing
1¼ cups (300 ml) sour cream
2 teaspoons coarse ground mustard
1 apple, finely cubed
sea salt flakes

1. Begin by blending together the ingredients for the dressing.

2. Drain the herring and cut into pieces. Slice the potatoes, and cut the beets into wedges.

3. Plate the salad, and distribute the potatoes, beets, and herring over the greens.

4. Melt the butter until it is lightly brown. Pour over the herring, potatoes, and beets.

5. Garnish with chives and serve with the dressing.

Beet Salad with Anchovies and Chive Cottage Cheese

A quickly made lunch salad, perfect for simple summer life. Freshly cooked new potatoes are a good addition if you would like a heartier meal.

4 portions

approx. 1¾ pounds (800 g) fresh beets
2 tins anchovies (each 1½ ounces/125 g)
2 thinly sliced spring onions
2 tablespoons freshly squeezed lemon juice
3 tablespoons canola oil
sea salt flakes
freshly ground white pepper
4 hardboiled eggs
½ cup (100 ml) chopped dill

Chive Cottage Cheese
9 ounces (250 g) cottage cheese
3 tablespoons chopped chives
1½ tablespoons coarse brown mustard

1. Begin by combining the ingredients for the chive cottage cheese.

2. Boil the beets until tender in lightly salted water. The time needed will depend on the size. Keep the root ends and a little of the stem as they will retain their color and taste better.

3. Rinse the beets under cold water, pull away the skin while they are warm, and cut into wedges.

4. Mix the anchovies, onions, lemon juice, and oil and spread over the beets. Add salt and pepper to taste. Top with halved hardboiled eggs, and garnish with chopped dill. Serve with the chive cottage cheese.

Root Vegetable Salad with Spelt And Venison Dip

In the summer we enjoy cool, light salads. But when the dark of winter comes, we would rather eat warmer and heavier food. Roasted root vegetables are always wonderful, and together with spelt berries and a tasty venison dip, this is a perfect autumn and winter salad.

4 portions

¾ cup (200 ml) spelt berries
2¼ pounds (1 kg) root vegetables such as beets, carrots, parsnips,
    celeriac, and rutabaga
2 red onions
2 tablespoons canola oil
1 tablespoon thyme
sea salt flakes
freshly ground pepper

Venison Dip
¼ pound (100 g) smoked venison steak, in thin slices
7 ounces (200 g) cream cheese, room temperature
4 ounces (125 g) quark or cottage cheese
2 teaspoons shredded horseradish or coarse brown mustard
¼ cup (50 ml) chopped chives
sea salt flakes
freshly ground pepper

1. **Begin with the Venison Dip:** Finely chop the meat. Mix with the rest of the ingredients and add salt and pepper to taste.

2. **The Salad:** Boil the spelt berries until tender, covered, according to the directions on the packaging for about 40 minutes. Add bouillon or salt toward the end of the cooking time. Drain any remaining water, and let the steam release.

3. Preheat the oven to 425°F (225°C). Brush the root vegetables clean. Peel the celeriac and rutabaga. Cut into smaller pieces. Peel and cut the onions into wedges. Lay everything out on a baking sheet lined with parchment paper, placing the beets apart. Mix with the oil, thyme, salt, and pepper.

4. Roast the root vegetables in the middle of the oven until tender, 25 to 30 minutes. Stir occasionally.

5. Combine the root vegetables with the spelt berries and serve with venison dip.

Cheddar Salad with Chorizo

It's time for some practical and prime salad tips. Always tear the lettuce leaves—that way you will have a higher yield than if you chop them. Afterward, lay the lettuce in ice cold water so it will become crispy. Let the lettuce drain well and dry it off. The leaves shouldn't be wet when they mix with the dressing. Consider mixing the salad with the dressing just before serving, otherwise the salad will be soft and limp.

4 portions

1 large head of iceberg lettuce
1 can chickpeas (14 ounces/400 g)
1 large red onion
9–10½ ounces (250–300 g) chorizo
oil for frying
peperoncini

Dressing
1 egg
1 garlic clove, pressed
1 tablespoon freshly squeezed lemon juice
2 teaspoons Dijon mustard
2 tablespoons water
⅔ cup (150 ml) canola oil
3½ ounces (100 g) finely grated cheddar cheese
sea salt flakes
freshly ground pepper

1. **Begin with the Dressing:** Combine the egg, garlic, lemon juice, mustard, and water. Pour in the oil in a fine stream and lastly add the cheese. Add salt and pepper to taste.

2. **The Salad:** Tear the lettuce leaves into smaller pieces. Ideally, lay it in ice water so it becomes crispy. Dry the leaves carefully.

3. Rinse the chickpeas and let drain. Peel and cut the onion in thin slices.

4. Cut the sausage into coins and fry in a small amount of oil. Let them drain on paper towels.

5. Mix together the lettuce, chickpeas, and the majority of the onion with the dressing. Make sure that all of the leaves are covered with dressing.

6. Top the salad with sausage, peperoncini, and the remainder of the onion.

Italian Bean Salad with Bresaola

Bresaola makes an excellent complement to this flavorful salad of grilled peppers, fennel, anchovies, and Parmesan cheese. Bresaola is an Italian meat that is salted and dried and has a more powerful taste than prosciutto.

4 portions

1 fennel bulb
1 red onion
9 ounces (250 g) cherry tomatoes
1 can roasted red peppers cut in strips, in oil (7 ounces/200 g)
1 can large white beans (14 ounces/400 g)
6 anchovy fillets
½–⅔ cup (100–150 ml) black olives
3 tablespoons olive oil
1 tablespoon red wine vinegar
2 teaspoons balsamic vinegar, preferably aged
sea salt flakes
freshly ground pepper
approx. 2 ounces (50 g) arugula
1 bunch of basil
Parmesan cheese

For Garnish
approx. ½ pound (200 g) bresaola

1. Slice the fennel and onion thinly. Halve the tomatoes. Drain the peppers. Rinse the beans in cold water and let drain. Cut the anchovies into small pieces.

2. Mix together the vegetables, beans, anchovies, olives, oil, and vinegar. Add salt and pepper to taste.

3. Fold in arugula and basil leaves just before serving.

4. Distribute the Parmesan generously over the salad and top with bresaola.

Sautéed Broccoli with Grilled Rib Eye

Sautéed broccoli with olive oil, chili, and garlic tastes much more exciting than just plain steamed broccoli. This is my favorite recipe for Friday nights—with a glass of red wine.

4 portions

1 pound (500 g) fresh broccoli
4 garlic cloves
1–2 dried chilies
⅓ cup (75 ml) olive oil
sea salt flakes
freshly ground pepper
4 rib eye steaks or sirloin

1. Divide the broccoli into florets, and cut the stalk into slices. Chop the garlic and chilies.

2. Lightly sauté the broccoli, garlic, and chilies in olive oil for about 5 minutes. Add salt to taste.

3. Grill the steaks over charcoal or on an indoor grill. Add salt and pepper to taste.

Minty Beans with Rack of Lamb

A warm bean salad with garlic, lemon, and mint adds a fresh new feeling to lamb chops.

4 portions

approx. 2 pounds (1 kg) rack of
  lamb or regular lamb chops
olive oil
sea salt flakes
freshly ground pepper

2 cans large white beans
  (each 14 ounces/400 g)
2 garlic cloves, chopped
1 lemon, zest and juice
3 tablespoons chopped fresh mint

1. Trim the meat and cut into chops. Rub with olive oil and grill the chops over charcoal or on an indoor grill. Add salt and pepper to taste.

2. Rinse the beans and let drain. Fry the beans and garlic in olive oil for a few minutes.

3. Mix in the lemon zest and juice. Add salt and pepper to taste and garnish with mint leaves.

New Potato Caesar with Crayfish and Prästost Cheese

Potato salad always tastes delicious. Here, I toss the freshly boiled new potatoes in a creamy Caesar dressing and top with crayfish, dill, and aged Prästost (Priest cheese; available from IKEA and stores with a well-stocked international cheese aisle). Shrimp, grilled chicken, smoked salmon, or other smoked fish are excellent additions.

4 portions

1¾ pounds (800 g) freshly boiled
    new potatoes
1¾ pounds (800 g) crayfish tails
2 tablespoons chopped dill
1 head romaine lettuce
approx. ¾ cup (200 ml) coarsely
    grated Prästost, Cheddar, or another
    strong cheese

Dressing
1 egg
2 anchovy fillets
½ lemon, juice
½ tablespoon Dijon mustard
½ teaspoon Worcestershire sauce
1 garlic clove, pressed
⅔ cup (150 ml) canola oil
¾ cup (200 ml) coarsely grated Prästost,
    Cheddar, or another strong cheese
½ tablespoon chopped dill
sea salt flakes
freshly ground pepper

1. **Begin with the Dressing:** Mix together all the ingredients with an immersion blender, except for the cheese and dill. Fold in the cheese and dill and add salt and pepper to taste.

2. **The Salad:** Cut the potatoes into smaller pieces and mix with the dressing. Mix the crayfish together with the dill.

3. Plate the romaine lettuce and distribute the potatoes over top. Garnish with crayfish and grated cheese.

Root Vegetable Omelet with Brie and Kale Salad

Kale, dried fruit, and nuts are delightful ingredients in a winter salad. A delicious omelet wih root vegetables and Brie are flavors that go well together, and make this a filling and unique salad plate.

4 portions

Omelet
approx. ¾ pounds (400 g) root
    vegetables such as carrots,
    celeriac, and parsnips
1 red pepper
1 red onion
canola oil
8 eggs
sea salt flakes
freshly ground pepper
½ cup (100 ml) chopped parsley
approx. 7 ounces (200 g) Brie cheese

Kale Salad
1 endive
2 fresh figs
1 ounce (25 g) walnuts
½ red onion
approx. 2 cups (500 ml) kale or spinach,
    rinsed and chopped
½ cup (100 ml) fresh dates, in pieces
3 tablespoons hazelnut or olive oil
2 tablespoons aged balsamic vinegar or
    crema di balsamico
sea salt flakes
freshly ground pepper

1. **The Omelet:** Preheat the oven to 425°F (225°C). Peel the root vegetables and cut them into 1-inch cubes. Cut the pepper into uniform pieces, peel and chop the onion.

2. Fry the vegetables in oil until tender. Let cool.

3. Whisk the eggs and add salt and pepper to taste. Fold in the vegetables and parsley.

4. Pour a little oil in a large frying pan that can withstand the heat of the oven. Pour in the omelet mixture. Let the omelet solidify on low heat without disturbing it.

5. Lay down slices of cheese when the omelet begins to solidify. Place the omelet in the middle of the oven for about 8 minutes. Cut the omelet into pieces and serve with the salad.

6. **The Salad:** Divide the endive leaves. Cut the figs into wedges. Break the nuts into smaller pieces. Peel and finely slice the onion.

7. Arrange the kale or spinach and endive on a large serving dish. Distribute the rest of the ingredients over top. Drizzle with oil and vinegar and add salt and pepper to taste.

Tomato Salad with Mozzarella Toast

Remember that the secret behind a good salad isn't just the salad itself but the quality of the ingredients. Use only sun-ripened tomatoes, the best olive oil, and high quality olives. In this classic caprese tomato salad, the foundation of tomatoes and mozzarella is irresistible. Here I have made my own heartier variant and I serve the tomato salad together with a delicious mozzarella toast.

4 portions

Salad
4 large ripe tomatoes
1 red onion
sea salt flakes
freshly ground pepper
¼ cup (50 ml) olive oil
½ cup (100 ml) black olives
two handfuls of arugula

Toast
2 mozzarella balls
approx. 2 ounces (50 g) thinly sliced salami
8 anchovy fillets
a few basil leaves
8 slices of sandwich bread (of the larger variety)
freshly ground pepper

1. **The Salad:** Slice the tomatoes and onion and arrange on a serving dish. Add salt and pepper to taste. Drizzle with olive oil. Top with the olives and arugula.

2. **The Toast:** Slice the mozzarella. Distribute mozzarella, salami, anchovies, and basil across four slices of bread. Add pepper to taste. Cover with the remaining bread.

3. Grill in a Panini press until the bread has browned and the cheese has melted. Cut the toast diagonally and serve hot with the salad.

Warm Salad with Tortellini and Arugula Dressing

Warm salad with tortellini, mushrooms, and nuts. Homemade pasta is even tastier and is easy to make.

4 portions

7 ounces (200 g) mushrooms
½ leek
olive oil
sea salt flakes
freshly ground pepper
1 head of romaine lettuce
¾–1 pound (500 g) fresh tortellini
¾ cup (200 ml) coarsely grated
    Parmesan cheese
¼ cup (50 ml) roasted pine nuts

Arugula Dressing
1 ounce (25 g) arugula
¾ cup (200 ml) light crème fraîche
    or sour cream
1 garlic clove, pressed
½ cup (100 ml) grated Parmesan cheese
sea salt flakes
freshly ground pepper

1. **Begin with the Dressing:** Chop the arugula. Mix together arugula, crème fraîche, and garlic. Add the cheese and add salt and pepper to taste.

2. **The Salad:** Slice the mushrooms and leek thinly and fry in a pan with olive oil. Add salt and pepper to taste.

3. Divide the romaine leaves.

4. Boil the pasta according to the directions on the packaging. Pour out the remaining water and blend the pasta with a couple of tablespoons of olive oil.

5. Combine the cooked pasta and romaine lettuce on plates. Top with mushrooms, cheese, and nuts. Serve with the dressing.

Quinoa Salad with Peaches, Goat Cheese, and Parma Ham

A salad with sun-ripened peaches is perfect for lazy summer days. An excellent substitute for the quinoa is 1¼ pounds (600 g) boiled new potatoes.

4 portions

¾ cup (200 ml) quinoa
2 peaches or nectarines
3½ ounces (100 g) sugar snap peas
3 tablespoons olive oil
½ lemon, zest and juice
1 bunch of basil
7 ounces (200 g) goat cheese (chèvre)
sea salt flakes
freshly ground pepper
1 head of leaf lettuce
¼–⅓ pound (100–150 g) Parma ham
    (or Prosciutto di Parma)

1. Boil the quinoa according to the directions on the packaging. Cut the peaches into wedges. Cut the pea pods into strips.

2. Blend quinoa, peaches, sugar snap peas, oil, lemon zest and juice. Carefully add the basil leaves and crumbled cheese. Add salt and pepper to taste.

3. Arrange the lettuce on a serving dish. Distribute the quinoa salad over the top and garnish with Parma ham.

Red Cabbage Salad with Chicken Kebab

Cabbage is a fantastic vegetable that many people overlook. In the winter be sure to revel in the variety of cabbage available. Together with feta cheese, dill, pomegranate, and spiced chicken kebab, this becomes a substantial salad with exciting flavors.

4 portions

Salad
½ head red cabbage
½ cup (100 ml) chopped dill
4 tablespoons olive oil
2 tablespoons red wine vinegar
freshly ground pepper
7 ounces (200 g) feta cheese
1 pomegranate

Chicken Kebab
¾–1 pound (400 g) chicken breast
2 teaspoons ground cumin
1 pinch cayenne pepper
1 tablespoon olive oil
1 garlic clove, pressed
sea salt flakes
4 short wooden skewers

1. **The Salad:** Cut the cabbage into fine strips with a cheese grater. Mix the cabbage with dill, oil, and vinegar. Add salt and pepper to taste.

2. Break the cheese into smaller pieces and add to the salad just before serving.

3. Halve the pomegranate and remove the seeds (with the shaft of a small spoon, for example). Remove the white pith. Distribute the seeds over the salad. Serve with freshly grilled chicken kebab.

4. **The Kebab:** Cut the chicken breast into small chunks. Mix together the spices, olive oil, garlic, and salt. Roll the chicken in the mixture.

5. Place the chicken on skewers. Cook the kebab on all sides in a nonstick frying pan, for about five minutes.

Glass Noodle Salad with Mango and Sesame Salmon

Simple noodle salad with fresh Asian flavors and fried salmon. A perfect and quickly made everyday meal, or maybe a fitting meal for when you have invited friends to dinner after work but don't have time to spend hours in the kitchen.

4 portions

5 ounces (150 g) glass noodles
1 mango
5 ounces (150 g) sugar snap peas
4 green onions
¼ cup (50 ml) chopped cilantro
1¼ pounds (600 g) salmon fillet
butter for frying
sea salt flakes
sesame seeds

Dressing
1 red chili pepper
2 tablespoons freshly squeezed lime juice
2 tablespoons Thai fish sauce
1 tablespoon canola oil
1 teaspoon sesame oil
1 teaspoon raw sugar
1 garlic clove, pressed

1. **Begin with the Dressing:** Split the chili pepper, scrape the seeds out and finely chop the chili. Mix together all of the ingredients.

2. **The Salad:** Boil lightly salted water in a pot. Remove from the heat and pour in the noodles. Cover and let the water absorb about three minutes (see the instructions on the packaging). Drain in a colander and rinse with cold water. Cut the noodles into smaller pieces with kitchen scissors.

3. Cut the mango into cubes and thinly slice the pea pods and the onions. Toss together the noodles, mango, sugar snap peas, onions, cilantro, and dressing.

4. Cut the salmon into cubes. Fry them quickly in a frying pan with butter. Add salt and pepper to taste and mix with sesame seeds. Distribute the salmon cubes over the noodle salad.

Parsnip Salad with Hazelnut Vinaigrette

In the early summer, try substituting the parsnips with asparagus. The green asparagus does need to be precooked—15 minutes in the oven.

4 portions

approx. 1 pound (500g) parsnips
approx. ¼ pound (150 g) Parma ham
    (or Prosciutto di Parma)
sea salt flakes
freshly ground pepper
1 can green lentils (14 ounces/400 g)
2 pears
1 head frisée lettuce
1 endive

Dressing
2 ounces (50 g) hazelnuts
2 tablespoons balsamic vinegar
4 tablespoons hazelnut- or walnut oil
sea salt flakes
freshly ground pepper

1. **The Dressing:** Roast the nuts in a dry, hot pan. Rub the shell of the nuts off between paper towels. Coarsely chop the nuts. Mix together the ingredients for the dressing.

2. Preheat the oven to 425°F (225°C). Peel the parsnips and cut into approximately 4-inch pieces. Lay them in water with lemon juice.

3. Boil the parsnips for about 6 minutes in lightly salted water or until just tender.

4. Cut the ham in slices lengthwise. Wrap a slice around every piece of parsnip. Lay on a baking sheet lined with parchment paper. Roast in the middle of the oven for about 15 minutes.

5. Rinse the lentils in cold water and let drain. Core the pears and cut into wedges.

6. Arrange the lettuce, endive, lentils, and pear on plates. Distribute the parsnips and add salt and pepper to taste. Drizzle with the dressing.

Roasted Mushroom Salad with Bacon

This rustic salad with roasted vegetables and bacon is just as delicious warm or cold. In the fall, it's always fun to use your own freshly picked mushrooms instead of store-bought ones.

4 portions

2 fennel bulbs
7 ounces (200 g) mushrooms
4 garlic cloves
2 red onions
3 tablespoons olive oil
1 pound (450 g) bacon
2 apples
1 can lentils (14 ounces/400 g)
½ orange, juice
sea salt flakes
freshly ground pepper
1 head frisée lettuce

1. Preheat the oven to 425°F (225°C). Cut the fennel bulbs into wedges and halve the mushrooms. Thinly slice the garlic and cut the red onions into wedges. Lay out the vegetables on a baking sheet lined with parchment paper. Drizzle with olive oil.

2. Roast in the middle of the oven for about 20 minutes.

3. Lay out the bacon on another baking sheet lined with parchment paper. Bake in the middle of the oven for about 10 minutes. Let drain on paper towels and break the bacon into smaller pieces.

4. If you have a convection oven, you can cook the vegetables and bacon at the same time on different baking sheets.

5. Rinse and cut the apples into wedges. Rinse the lentils and let drain.

6. Mix together the vegetables, apples, lentils, and orange juice. Add salt and pepper to taste.

7. Arrange the salad on a serving plate with the frisée lettuce. Top with bacon.

Spring Vegetable Salad with Smoked Fish and Egg

Delightful summer salads with spring vegetables such as asparagus and new potatoes go really well with smoked fish. The salad is also delicious when topped with smoked shrimp.

4 portions

2 eggs
½ pound (250 g) green asparagus
½ pound (200 g) boiled new
    potatoes, cooled
1 red onion
1 bunch of radishes
½ cucumber
1 small head iceberg lettuce
⅔–¾ pound (300–400 g) cleaned
    whitefish, kippers, or mackerel
¼ cup (50 ml) chopped dill

Dressing
3 tablespoons cold-pressed canola oil
2 tablespoons freshly squeezed lemon juice
1 tablespoon shredded horseradish
sea salt flakes

1. Begin by mixing together the ingredients for the dressing.

2. Boil the eggs for approximately 6 minutes. The yolk should preferably be left creamy. Rinse in cold water and slice the egg neatly in half.

3. Cut away the coarse lower portion of the asparagus. Boil it until tender in lightly salted water for about 5 minutes. Cool the asparagus in cold water.

4. Cut the asparagus in half and cut the potatoes into smaller pieces. Thinly slice the onion and radishes. Roughly peel the cucumber. Cut it lengthwise, scrape out the seeds, and cut into slices. Tear the lettuce into smaller pieces.

5. Mix together lettuce, potatoes, and vegetables. Drizzle with dressing and toss together. Lay the fish and eggs on top, and garnish with dill.

Eggplant Salad with Halloumi

A filling salad that elicits thoughts of warm Mediterranean evenings. I top the salad with grilled halloumi and eat it as an entrée; however, the salad is also an outstanding accompaniment to grilled lamb or chicken.

4 portions

¼ cup (50 ml) pine nuts
5 tomatoes
1 eggplant
1 squash
3 garlic cloves
14 ounces (400 g) wheat berries
olive oil for frying
½ lemon, zest
sea salt flakes
freshly ground pepper
approx. 2 ounces (50 g) arugula
approx. 10½ ounces (300 g) halloumi

1. Roast the pine nuts in a dry pan.

2. Cut the tomatoes, eggplant, and squash into cubes. Peel and chop the garlic. Rinse the wheat berries and let drain.

3. Fry the eggplant, squash, and garlic in olive oil until the vegetables are tender. Fold in tomatoes, wheat berries, and lemon zest and fry an additional few minutes. Add salt and pepper to taste.

4. Add the arugula just before serving and garnish with nuts.

5. Cut the cheese into slices and fry both sides quickly in olive oil. Serve the cheese fresh out of the pan with the warm salad.

Warm Fennel Salad with Oven-Baked Salmon

Baking a whole salmon fillet in the oven is very practical. The fennel's mild anise flavor is a good complement to the salmon, and the apple gives it a fruity crispness. In the early summer, when it's spring vegetable time, the fennel can be replaced with green asparagus. Simply remove the lower, rougher part of the asparagus stalks, slice the stalks down the middle, and fry them in the same way as the fennel.

4 portions

1¾ pounds (800 g) salmon fillet
sea salt flakes
freshly ground pepper
2 tablespoons olive oil

Salad
¾ cup (200 ml) quinoa
1 vegetable bouillon cube
2 large fennel bulbs
2 green apples
olive oil
sea salt flakes
freshly ground pepper
½ lemon, juice
½ cup (100 ml) chopped dill

1. Preheat the oven to 350°F (175°C). Lay the salmon on a greased oven-safe dish. Add salt and pepper to taste, and drizzle with olive oil. Bake in the middle of the oven for about 20 minutes. Remove and cover with foil.

2. **The Salad:** Cook the quinoa in bouillon according to the instructions on the packaging. Let the steam release.

3. Chop the fennel into wedges. Remove the apple cores and cut apples into thin wedges; place the apples in a bowl with lemon water so they don't brown.

4. Fry the fennel in olive oil for about 5 minutes until tender. Add apple wedges and continue to fry a couple of minutes. Add salt and pepper to taste and squeeze the lemon on top. Fold the quinoa and dill into the fried fennel.

5. Fill the bottoms of four deep-dish plates with salad, lay the salmon pieces on top, and top it off with a couple of turns of the pepper mill.

Pork Tenderloin with Warm Feta Cheese Salad

This warm salad with Greek flavors served with marinated pork tenderloin is easy to make and feels like luxury.

4 portions

approx. 1¼ pounds (600 g) pork tenderloin
3 tablespoons olive oil
1 lemon, zest
2 teaspoons veal stock
freshly ground pepper
sea salt flakes
lemon for garnish

Salad
1 cucumber
4 tomatoes
1 red onion
olive oil for frying
½ cup (100 ml) kalamata olives
1 bunch of basil
sea salt flakes
freshly ground pepper
5 ounces (150 g) feta cheese

1. **The Meat:** Trim the tenderloin free of fat and tendons. Slice into approximately 1-inch-thick medallions.

2. In a large bowl, mix together the olive oil, lemon zest, stock, and freshly ground pepper. Add the meat and let it marinate for about two hours.

3. Fry or grill the meat for 2 to 3 minutes per side. Add salt to taste. Serve the meat with salad and lemon wedges.

4. **The Salad:** Split the cucumber lengthwise, scrape out the seeds with a spoon, and cut into slices. Roughly chop the tomatoes. Peel and cut the onion into wedges.

5. Fry the cucumber and onion in olive oil over low heat for a couple of minutes. Add the tomatoes and fry an additional few minutes. Add the olives and basil leaves. Add salt and pepper to taste. Top with crumbled cheese.

Barley Salad with Roasted Beets and Pork Belly

Barley and pork belly are a classic combination. Making a salad using these popular ingredients is a good way to update this everyday favorite. However, consider buying whole grain barley as crushed barley has a texture a little more like porridge.

4 portions

¾ cup (200 ml) hull-less barley
approx. 1 pound (500 g) beets
1½ tablespoons canola oil
¼ cup (50 ml) fresh thyme, with stems removed
sea salt flakes
freshly ground pepper
approx. 7 ounces (200 g) lightly salted pork belly
⅔ cup (150 ml) leek, cut in thin strips
1 head frisée lettuce
3 tablespoons canola oil
2 tablespoons aged balsamic vinegar or crema di balsamico
approx. 3 ounces (75 g) aged cheese

1. Boil the hull-less barley according to the instructions on the packaging. Pour out the excess water, and let the steam release from the barley.

2. Preheat the oven to 425°F (225°C). Brush the beets clean and cut them into wedges. Lay them out on a baking sheet lined with parchment paper and coat with the olive oil.

3. Roast the beets in the middle of the oven until they are tender, 25 to 30 minutes. Stir occasionally. Mix the beets with thyme, salt, and pepper.

4. Cut the pork into strips and fry until crispy. Let drain on a double layer of paper towels.

5. Combine the barley and leeks.

6. Arrange lettuce, barley, and beets on a serving dish. Add salt and pepper to taste. Distribute the pork over the salad, drizzle with oil and vinegar, and garnish with shredded cheese.

Halloumi Potatoes with Lamb Kebab

Dill, almonds, pecorino, and chili. Could this Mediterranean-inspired salad be anything other than delicious? And with halloumi in the salad, it's only natural to add lamb.

4 portions

Kebab
1¼ pounds (600 g) boneless lamb steak
3 tablespoons olive oil
½ lemon, zest and juice
2 garlic cloves, pressed
2 teaspoons oregano
3 tablespoons chopped dill
sea salt flakes
freshly ground pepper
wooden skewers

Potato Salad
2¼ pounds (1 kg) new potatoes
½ cup (100 ml) almonds
1 garlic clove, chopped
¾ cup (200 ml) chopped dill
1 lemon, juice
½ cup (100 ml) olive oil
sea salt flakes
freshly ground pepper
3½ ounces (100 g) coarsely grated halloumi
1 red chili, cut into strips
½ pound (250 g) cherry tomatoes

1. **The Kebab:** Trim and cut the meat into approximately 1-inch cubes.

2. Combine together olive oil, lemon juice, garlic, oregano, and dill. Add in the meat and let marinate for a minimum of two hours.

3. Place the meat on skewers. Grill over charcoal, turning to cook all sides, and add salt and pepper to taste.

4. **The Potato Salad:** Wash the potatoes and cook in lightly salted water until tender. Let chill. Roughly chop the potatoes.

5. **The Pesto:** Blend together almonds, garlic, dill, lemon juice, olive oil, salt, and pepper.

6. Fold the potatoes into the pesto.

7. Fold in halloumi, strips of chili, and halved cherry tomatoes just before serving.

Creamy Lentils with Smoked Mussels and Bacon

Surely we can all call lentils and canned beans the world's best fast food. Just open, rinse, and add the flavor you like. In this creamy lentil salad, there's a meeting of many exciting flavors. What do you say to mussels, ruby red grapefruit, bacon, and flavorful mustard dressing?

4 portions

Salad
2 cans green lentils
 (each 14 ounces/400 g)
5 ounces (140 g) bacon
2 ounces (50 g) baby spinach
2 ruby red grapefruit
2 stalks celery
2 avocadoes
½ cup (100 ml) leeks,
 cut into strips
1 tin of smoked mussels
 (approx. 3½ ounces/100 g)

Dressing
1 egg yolk
1½ tablespoons Dijon mustard
½ cup (100 ml) Greek yogurt
¼ cup (50 ml) canola oil
⅓ cup (75 ml) chopped dill
sea salt flakes
freshly ground pepper

1. **Begin with the Dressing:** Mix together the egg yolk, mustard, and yogurt. Pour in the oil in a fine stream. Mix in the dill and add salt and pepper to taste.

2. **The Salad:** Rinse the lentils and let drain. Combine the lentils with the dressing.

3. Cut the bacon into strips and fry until crispy. Drain on paper towels.

4. Rinse the spinach and dry off the leaves carefully. Peel the grapefruit with a knife so the white pith is removed. Cut out the skin-free wedges between the membranes of the grapefruit. Cut the celery into strips. Halve the avocadoes and remove the pits. Scrape out the avocado in pieces with a teaspoon.

5. Fold in the spinach, celery, avocado, leeks, mussels, and most of the grapefruit into the lentils.

6. Garnish with the rest of the grapefruit wedges and top with bacon.

Caviar Potatoes with Gravlax

The summer's most luxurious potato salad! Superb with gravlax but also a great addition to the poached salmon on page 123.

4 portions

1¾ pounds (800 g) cooked, cold new potatoes
1¼ cups (300 ml) sour cream
4 ounces (100 g) caviar
½ cup (100 ml) finely chopped red onion
½ cup (100 ml) chopped dill
sea salt flakes
freshly ground white pepper

For Serving
approx. 14 ounces (400 g) gravlax

1. Cut the potatoes into smaller pieces.

2. Combine sour cream, caviar, onion, dill, salt, and pepper. Fold in the potatoes.

3. Plate the potato salad and top with a little extra red onion and dill. Serve together with the gravlax.

Salad with Peaches and Ham Toast au Gratin

A warm sandwich with ham and goat cheese goes well with this substantial salad with whole oat groats and peaches.

4 portions

¾ cup (200 ml) whole oat groats
1¾ cup (400 ml) water
1 chicken bouillon cube
1 small red onion
2 peaches
2 tomatoes
¼ cup (50 ml) olive oil
2 tablespoons balsamic vinegar
sea salt flakes
freshly ground pepper
3½ ounces (100 g) arugula
4 slices Danish rye bread
4 slices smoked ham
7 ounces (200 g) goat cheese (chèvre)

1. Boil the whole oat groats in bouillon according to the instructions on the packaging for about 12 minutes. Let cool.

2. Peel and thinly slice the onion. Chop the peaches and tomatoes into pieces.

3. Combine oil, vinegar, salt, and pepper in a large bowl. Fold the whole oat groats, onion, peaches, tomatoes, and arugula into the dressing just before serving. Lay out onto plates.

4. Preheat the oven to 475°F (250°C). Place the ham on the bread and the cheese on top, on a baking sheet covered with parchment paper.

5. Bake in the upper part of the oven for approximately 4 minutes. Divide each slice into quarters and lay them out onto the salad.

Toast au Chèvre Chaud with Pear Salad

A French classic that never gets old. Here I've chosen to serve it with goat cheese au gratin on a dark rye bread; however, a whole grain sandwich bread is also a good choice.

4 portions

The Toast
4 slices Danish rye bread
2 ounces (50 g) goat cheese (chèvre)
2 ounces (50 g) walnuts
2 tablespoons honey

The Salad
approx. 2 cups (500 ml) frisée or
    radicchio lettuce
2 celery stalks
1 pear
3 tablespoons hazelnut oil
1½ tablespoons crema di balsamico
sea salt flakes
freshly ground pepper

1. **The Toast:** Preheat the oven to 425°F (225°C). Toast the bread slices. Cut off the crusts to form a square or cut a circle out using a glass.

2. Place one slice of cheese on each bread slice and place them on a baking sheet line with parchment paper. Lay the nuts on the side.

3. Place in the middle of the oven until the cheese begins to melt and the nuts gain a nice color, approximately 7 minutes. Watch the nuts carefully so they don't burn.

4. Drizzle honey over the cheese while it's still warm.

5. **The Salad:** Arrange the toast on the lettuce together with strips of celery, sliced pear, and nuts. Drizzle with oil and vinegar, and add salt and pepper to taste.

Cheddar Salad with Kamut Wheat and Venison

The available grain and seed options have really exploded in recent years! For this warm salad, I've used kamut wheat, which you can read more about on page 191. Feel free to try it with wheat berries, spelt berries, hull-less barley, or pearl barley.

4 portions

1 cup (250 ml) kamut wheat
1 zucchini
5 ounces (150 g) haricots verts (or green beans)
1 red onion
butter for frying
sea salt flakes
freshly ground pepper
3 tablespoons capers
½ cup (100 ml) chopped dill
¾ cup (200 ml) coarsely grated cheddar cheese
approx. ½ pound (200 g) sliced smoked venison

Horseradish Cream
3½ ounces (100 g) cream cheese
9 ounces (250 g) quark or cottage cheese
2–3 teaspoons grated horseradish
sea salt flakes

1. Begin by combining the ingredients for the horseradish cream.

2. Boil the kamut wheat according to the instructions on the packaging. Add bouillon or salt toward the end of the cooking time. Pour out excess water and let the steam release.

3. Cut the zucchini into small cubes and the beans into smaller pieces. Peel and chop the onion. Fry the vegetables until tender in a pan. Add salt and pepper to taste.

4. Blend the wheat with vegetables, capers, and dill and add salt and pepper to taste. Fold in the cheese just before serving. Serve the salad with smoked venison and horseradish cream.

Pepper Strawberries with Goat Cheese Chicken

This salad is a real home run with this goat cheese gratinated chicken, but it also goes great with a grilled pork loin. Simply a perfect salad for the summer's comfortable evenings and easy-going parties.

4 portions

4 chicken breasts (approx. 1 pound/500 g)
butter for frying
sea salt flakes
freshly ground pepper
approx. 7 ounces (200 g) goat cheese
    (chèvre), packaged in a roll
1 tablespoon chopped fresh rosemary
2 tablespoons honey
1 quart (1 liter) strawberries
2 avocadoes
2 tablespoons white wine vinegar
⅓ cup (75 ml) grapeseed oil
30 mint leaves
2 ounces (50 g) maché lettuce

1. Preheat the oven to 425°F (225°C). Brown the chicken breasts in butter, about 10 minutes per side. Add salt and pepper to taste and place the breasts on a baking sheet covered with parchment paper.

2. Place one slice of goat cheese on each breast, sprinkle with rosemary, and drizzle with honey. Bake in the middle of the oven for about 10 minutes.

3. Clean and cut the strawberries into wedges. Peel and slice the avocadoes.

4. Toss strawberries, avocadoes, vinegar, oil, ½ teaspoon freshly crushed pepper, and salt. Fold in the mint and lettuce.

Smoked Salmon with Melon and Egg Hummus

A summer salad with melon and radishes is a fresh look and a good addition to the powerful flavor of smoked salmon. Here I serve salad and hummus together with cold smoked salmon, but warmed smoked salmon, kippers, or pepper mackerel are also good accompaniments.

4 portions

approx. 14 ounces (400 g) thinly sliced cold smoked salmon
1 lemon

Melon Salad
1 small melon (approx. 1½ pounds/700 g)
1 bunch of radishes
1 fennel bulb
2 tablespoons chopped dill
2 tablespoons chopped chives
2 tablespoons freshly squeezed lemon juice
3 tablespoons canola oil
sea salt flakes
freshly ground pepper
Boston lettuce

Egg Hummus
1 can chickpeas (14 ounces/400 g)
½ cup (100 ml) Greek yogurt
1 teaspoon Dijon mustard
2 tablespoons freshly squeezed lemon juice
3 hardboiled eggs
¼ cup (50 ml) chopped red onion
3 tablespoons chopped dill
a dash of Tabasco
sea salt flakes

1. **Hummus:** Rinse the chickpeas and let drain. Combine chickpeas, yogurt, mustard, and lemon juice. Peel and mash the egg with a fork. Add in eggs, onion, and dill. Season with Tabasco and salt to taste.

2. **The Salad:** Halve the melon, cut back the rind, scrape out the seeds, and cut into smaller pieces. Wash the radishes and slice them thinly. Halve the fennel and slice thinly.

3. Mix together melon, radishes, fennel, herbs, lemon juice, and oil. Add salt and pepper to taste.

4. Arrange the Boston lettuce on a serving dish. Distribute the melon salad on top. Serve with smoked salmon, hummus, and lemon wedges.

Cauliflower with Bleu Cheese and Turkey

Smoked meat is a safe bet for the summertime. This distinctive salad is just as delicious with ham as it is with smoked turkey breast. Serve at room temperature or cold.

4 portions

1¼ cups (300 ml) sour cream
1 tablespoon Dijon mustard
½ cup (100 ml) chopped chives
sea salt flakes
freshly ground white pepper
1 large or 2 small cauliflower heads
5 ounces (150 g) bleu cheese
3 tablespoons roasted sunflower seeds
approx. ½ pound (200 g) smoked turkey breast or ham

1. Mix together sour cream, mustard, and most of the chives. Add salt and pepper to taste.

2. Divide the cauliflower head into florets. Boil some lightly salted water, place in the cauliflower florets, and cook, covered, until tender. Pour out the remaining water.

3. Arrange the cauliflower on a serving dish. Drizzle the dressing on top, garnishing with crumbled cheese, sunflower seeds, and chives. Serve the salad together with the smoked turkey.

Spicy Sausage with Warm Beet Salad

You can never have too many tasty recipes! For me, spicy sausage with pickled beets is yummy. However, I am also crazy about fresh beets and often make this beet salad with horseradish to accompany spicy sausage. The warm beet salad also goes well with sausages that have a mild flavor, like grilled hot dogs, or similar.

4 portions

Beet Salad
1 pound (500 g) beets
1 tablespoon canola oil
sea salt flakes
freshly ground pepper
¾ cup (200 ml) pearl barley
1 vegetable bouillon cube
2 ounces (50 g) delicate salad shoots such as red chard

Dressing
¼ cup (50 ml) canola oil
1½ tablespoons freshly squeezed lemon juice
1½ tablespoons shredded horseradish
2 tablespoons chopped chives
1 tablespoon water
sea salt flakes

For Serving
spicy sausage

1. Begin by blending together the ingredients for the dressing.

2. Preheat the oven to 425°F (225°C). Brush the beets clean and cut into wedges. Lay them out on a baking sheet lined with parchment paper and mix together with oil, salt, and pepper.

3. Roast for about 25 to 30 minutes in the middle of the oven until the beets are tender.

4. Boil the pearl barley in bouillon, covered, according to the directions on the packaging, for about 8 minutes. Let the steam evaporate.

5. Toss the beets with the dressing. Fold in the barley and salad shoots just before serving. Serve the salad together with freshly fried sausage.

Melon and Ham with Chive-Tossed Potatoes

This is an easy summer recipe when you want to eat well but still want to spend more time outside than in the kitchen. The fresh melon salad with chive and tossed new potatoes is perfect to serve with cold cuts like ham or turkey. The mint can also be substituted with fresh basil.

4 portions

Melon Salad
approx. 2¼ pounds (1 kg) melon
1 tablespoon freshly squeezed lemon juice
2 tablespoons canola oil
3 tablespoons chopped fresh mint

Chive-Tossed New Potatoes
2¼ pounds (1 kg) new potatoes
3½ tablespoons (50 g) butter
approx. ¾ cup (200 ml) chopped chives

For Serving
approx. ½ pound (200 g) thinly sliced ham or smoked turkey breast

1. **The Salad:** Slice the melon into smaller pieces and combine with lemon juice, oil, and mint.

2. **The Potatoes:** Brush the potatoes clean and boil in lightly salted water until tender. Let the steam release.

3. Melt the butter and add the chives. Pour the herbed butter over the potatoes and toss. Serve immediately with the melon salad and ham.

Fennel Salad with Whole Barley and Crayfish

Barley is a terrific grain to use in salads. Plan on buying whole barleycorn as crushed barley has a tendency to become like gruel. I prefer to use pearl barley, which is grain cut up into smaller pieces. The salad is also excellent when topped with warm smoked salmon.

4 portions

¾ cup (200 ml) whole hull-less barley
1 vegetable bouillon cube
1 fennel bulb
3 ounces (75 g) sugar snap peas
4 green onions
2 ounces (50 g) baby spinach
½ cup (100 ml) chopped dill
1 lemon, zest and juice
2 tablespoons canola oil
sea salt flakes
freshly ground pepper
1¾ pounds (800 g) crayfish tails
approx. ¾ cup (200 ml) grated cheddar cheese

1. Boil the barley, covered, according to the instructions on the packaging. Add bouillon or salt toward the end of the cooking time. Pour out the excess water and let the steam release.

2. Thinly slice the fennel, sugar snap peas, and onions. Rinse the spinach and dry the leaves carefully.

3. Fold fennel, sugar snap peas, onion, spinach, dill, lemon, and oil into the barley. Add salt and pepper to taste.

4. Plate the salad and top with crayfish and grated cheddar.

Potato Salad with Smoked Salmon and Shrimp

In the summer, I can't get enough of these wonderful salads that feature new potatoes. For me, smoked fish is also standard summer fare, so what could be more summery than a potato salad with smoked salmon and shrimp? Considering smoked fish has a fairly strong flavor, fruit makes a fresh and welcome addition to the salad. Here I've used melon, but nectarines or pears are also excellent.

4 portions

1 pound (500 g) new potatoes
½ lemon, zest and juice
2 tablespoons olive oil
¼ cup (50 ml) chopped dill
sea salt flakes
freshly ground white pepper
1 pound (500 g) shrimp, unpeeled
⅔–¾ pound (300–400 g) smoked salmon
½ of a small melon (approx. ¾ pound/400 g)
3½ ounces (100 g) sugar snap peas
2 red onions
Boston lettuce
lemon wedges for garnish

Dressing
3 ounces (75 g) frozen chopped spinach
½ cup (100 ml) chopped dill
1 garlic clove, pressed
¾ cup (200 ml) Greek yogurt
1 teaspoon Dijon mustard
sea salt flakes
freshly ground white pepper

1. Boil the potatoes in lightly salted water. Let the steam release and cut the potatoes in half.

2. Combine the lemon, olive oil, dill, salt, and pepper. Toss the potatoes with the dressing from step six and let chill.

3. Peel and cook shrimp. Cut the salmon into smaller pieces.

4. Cut the pulp of the melon into smaller pieces. Thinly slice the pea pods and onions.

5. Lay the lettuce on a serving dish. Top with the potato salad, salmon, and shrimp. Serve with lemon wedges and dressing.

6. **The Dressing:** Thaw the spinach. Drain through a sieve and press out all the liquid. Mix together all ingredients. Add salt and pepper to taste.

Lingonberry and Red Cabbage Salad with Black Pudding

A scrumptious raw salad with lingonberries, apple, and walnuts gilds this delicious black pudding.

4 portions

approx. 1 pound (500 g) red cabbage
1 apple
2 tablespoons crema di balsamico
2 tablespoons hazelnut oil
2 ounces (50 g) coarsely chopped walnuts
¾ cup (200 ml) frozen lingonberries
    or cranberries
sea salt flakes
freshly ground pepper

For Serving
approx. 2 pounds (850 g) black pudding
butter for frying

1. Cut the cabbage into thin strips with a cheese grater. Rinse the apple and cut into wedges.

2. Combine all the ingredients for the salad in a large bowl and add salt and pepper to taste.

3. Slice the black pudding and fry in butter until crisp. Serve with the red cabbage salad.

Ham Salad with Chutney and Black Pudding

Black pudding is excellent. With additions like ham salad and pear chutney, it becomes the quintessential luxury meal!

4 portions

approx. ½ pound (200 g) smoked ham, in pieces
1 head iceberg lettuce
3 tablespoons canola oil
1½ tablespoons white wine vinegar
sea salt flakes
freshly ground pepper
1 pear
¼ cup (50 ml) mango chutney

For Serving
2 pounds (850 g) black pudding
butter for frying

1. Cut the ham into thin sticks and break the lettuce into smaller pieces. Blend together oil and vinegar and add salt and pepper to taste.

2. Mix the lettuce with the ham and the dressing just before serving.

3. Cut the pear into small cubes and mix together with the mango chutney.

4. Slice the black pudding and fry in butter until crisp. Serve with ham salad and pear chutney.

Creamy Potato Salad with Poached Salmon

Poached salmon is a classic shared meal that is always easy to prepare—and it is always popular! Serve preferably with melon wedges, as they serve both as a lovely garnish and as a good accompaniment to the poached fish. The creamy potato salad makes it so that no extra sauce is needed. The potato salad is also a good addition to cold cuts, grilled and smoked fish.

4 portions

Salmon
½ leek
1 fennel bulb
1 lemon
4½ cups (1 liter) water
1 tablespoon white wine vinegar
dill sprigs
1 tablespoon salt
4 boneless salmon fillets with skin
    (approx. 1¼ pounds/600 g)

Potato Salad
2 egg yolks
1 teaspoon freshly squeezed lemon juice
2 teaspoons Dijon mustard
½ cup (100 ml) chopped dill
⅔ cup (150 ml) canola oil
2 tablespoons water
sea salt flakes
freshly ground white pepper
2¼ pounds (1 kg) cooked, cold new potatoes
1 small red onion, chopped
3 tablespoons chopped chives

1. **The Salmon:** Slice the leek into smaller pieces. Slice the fennel and the lemon thinly.

2. Boil water, vinegar, dill sprigs, and salt in a frying pan. Add the leek, fennel, and lemon. Cook, covered, for about 10 minutes.

3. Place the salmon into the pan and cook on low heat, covered, about 12 minutes. Let the salmon cool in the marinade. Garnish with lemon and dill just before serving.

4. **The Salad:** Mix egg yolks, lemon juice, mustard, and dill with an immersion blender. Drizzle the oil in slowly and mix until it is a thick cream. Add in the water and add salt and pepper to taste.

5. Cut the potatoes into smaller pieces. Carefully fold the potatoes into the sauce. Arrange the potatoes and garnish with red onion and chives.

Mezze Platter

Mezze are small dishes from the Eastern Mediterranean region. Arrange all the ingredients in bowls by themselves and let everyone create their own plate of delicacies truly worthy of that Arabian Nights–feeling.

My mezze platter for 4 people
Fattoush Hummus
Tzatziki, page 18
20 ounces (560 g) stuffed grape leaves
Pepperoncini
Olives

Fattoush

Fattoush is a hearty farmer's salad with toasted pita bread. The salad can, as shown here, be served on the mezze table but also is a wonderful accompaniment to grilled lamb or chicken.

4 portions

2 pieces pita bread
olive oil for frying
1 cucumber
4 tomatoes
1 yellow pepper
1 red onion
½ cup (100 ml) chopped parsley
¼ cup (50 ml) chopped mint
1 tablespoon freshly squeezed lemon juice
3 tablespoons olive oil
2 garlic cloves, pressed
sea salt flakes
freshly ground pepper

1. Cut the bread into small pieces and fry in olive oil.

2. Halve and deseed the cucumber and tomatoes. Remove the seeds from the pepper, and peel the onion. Slice the vegetables into small pieces.

3. Blend together vegetables, herbs, lemon juice, olive oil, and garlic. Add salt and pepper to taste. Preferably, let the flavor develop a bit before the salad is served.

4. Fold the bread into the salad just before serving.

Hummus

Known as "Middle Eastern butter," hummus is one of the most common mezze and is a perfect dip to go with most foods.

4 portions

1 can chickpeas (14 ounces/400 g)
2 garlic cloves
1 lemon, juice
⅓ cup (75 ml) olive oil
¼ teaspoon ground cumin
1 tablespoon tahini (sesame paste)
sea salt flakes
freshly ground pepper

1. Rinse the chickpeas in cold water and let drain.

2. Blend together all the ingredients until consistency is smooth and add salt and pepper to taste.

Oriental Bulgur with Halloumi

A juicy bulgur salad that has the exciting taste of apricots, mint, and pistachios. The finishing touch is beautiful pomegranate seeds. I serve this delicious salad as an entrée with grilled halloumi and yogurt sauce. It is also a standard winter salad that I love to include on my Christmas table, but then I omit the halloumi and yogurt sauce.

4 portions

1 pomegranate
1 vegetable bouillon cube
2 cups (500 ml) water
½ g saffron
1 garlic clove, pressed
1 teaspoon harissa
1 teaspoon freshly crushed cardamom pods
1 cup (250 ml) bulgur
1 can chickpeas (14 ounces/400 g)
2 tablespoons olive oil
approx. ¾ cup (200 ml) dried fruit,
    cut into pieces, such as apricots,
    figs, dates, raisins, prunes
½ cup (100 ml) coarsely
    chopped pistachios
4 tablespoons chopped mint
approx. 10½ ounces (300 g) halloumi

Yogurt Sauce
¾ cup (200 ml) Greek yogurt
1 garlic clove, pressed
½ teaspoon ground cumin
sea salt flakes

1. Begin by combining the ingredients for the yogurt sauce.

2. Halve the pomegranate and remove the seeds and the white pith.

3. Bring to a boil the bouillon, water, saffron, garlic, harissa, and cardamom. Add the bulgur and cook, covered, for about 10 minutes.

4. Rinse the chickpeas and let drain.

5. Remove the pot from the burner, let the steam release, and fluff with a fork. Combine with the chickpeas, olive oil, fruits, nuts, and mint. Plate, and top with pomegranate seeds.

6. Slice the halloumi and fry in olive oil. Serve the salad with freshly fried halloumi and yogurt sauce.

Root Vegetable Salad with Spelt Berries and Kale Pesto

Adding whole grains to a salad is both delicious and nutritious. I use spelt, but if time is scarce there are alternatives which have shorter cooking times, for example, wheat berries, pearl barley, or precooked kamut berries. A winter pesto made of kale, cheddar cheese, and almonds completes the salad.

4 portions

Root Vegetable Salad
¾ cup (200 ml) spelt berries
1 vegetable bouillon cube
1¾ cup (400 ml) water
2¼ pounds (1 kg) root vegetables such as carrots, beets, parsnips, celeriac, and rutabaga
2 red onions
2 tablespoons canola oil
2 tablespoons chopped fresh rosemary
sea salt flakes
freshly ground pepper
approx. 3 ounces (75 g) grated cheddar cheese

Pesto
½ cup (100 ml) almonds
1 garlic clove
¾ cup (200 ml) kale or spinach, rinsed and cut into strips
½ cup (100 ml) coarsely grated cheddar cheese
½ cup (100 ml) canola oil
sea salt flakes
freshly ground pepper

1. **Begin with the Pesto:** Blend almonds, garlic, and kale or spinach. Add in the cheese and lastly the oil. Add salt and pepper to taste.

2. **The Salad:** Boil the spelt berries, covered, according to the directions on the packaging, for about 40 minutes. Add bouillon or salt toward the end of the cooking time. Drain excess water and let the steam release.

3. Preheat the oven to 425°F (225°C). Brush the root vegetables clean, peel the celeriac and rutabaga. Cut into smaller pieces. Peel and cut the onions into wedges. Lay everything out on a baking sheet lined with parchment paper, placing the beets separately. Sprinkle with oil, rosemary, salt, and pepper.

4. Roast the root vegetables in the middle of the oven until they are tender, 25 to 30 minutes. Stir occasionally.

5. Combine the root vegetables and spelt, and add salt and pepper to taste. Top with grated cheddar cheese and serve with the pesto.

Thai Salad with Lamb Tenderloin

A filling salad with a delightful Thai flavor. Originally, the salad was made with beef, but I love lamb and find lamb tenderloin a practical alternative. Sometimes I make an everyday variant with store-bought roast beef. I usually get it sliced extra thin so it feels juicier. Calculate approximately half a pound for four people.

4 portions

approx. 1 pound (500 g) lamb tenderloin
peanut oil
sea salt flakes
freshly ground pepper

Dressing
2 red chilies
2 tablespoons Thai fish sauce
2 tablespoons freshly squeezed lime
2 teaspoons raw sugar

Salad
½ cucumber
1 papaya
4¼ cups (1 liter) tender lettuce leaves
½ cup (100 ml) chopped cilantro
¼ cup (50 ml) Thai basil, cut into strips
¼ cup (50 ml) chopped mint
½ cup (100 ml) leeks, cut into strips
½ cup (100 ml) coarsely chopped cashews

1. **The Dressing:** Divide the chili peppers lengthwise, and coarsely scrape out the seeds, preferably leaving a few in to add a bit of zing to the flavor. Finely chop the chilies and combine together the ingredients for the dressing.

2. **The Meat:** Brown the meat on all sides in oil. Reduce the temperature and continue frying a couple of minutes. The meat should still be pink inside. Add salt and pepper to taste. Wrap the meat in aluminum foil and let rest for about 10 minutes.

3. **The Salad:** Cut the cucumber lengthwise, scrape out the seeds, and cut into thin slices. Peel and cut the papaya into cubes. Arrange the lettuce leaves, cucumber, papaya, and herbs onto plates.

4. Slice the meat into thin slices and distribute atop the salad. Drizzle with dressing and garnish with leeks and nuts.

Lentil Salad with Mozzarella and Mango

Tomatoes and mozzarella are a classic combination, but when it isn't tomato season, mango is a very good alternative. Or, try persimmons, which are also a delicious winter fruit. Lentils make the salad substantial and for those who would like a vegetarian salad, simply omit the ham.

4 portions

2 cans green lentils (each 14 ounces/400 g)
1 red chili pepper
1 garlic clove, pressed
¼ cup (50 ml) chopped sun-dried tomatoes
1 tablespoon balsamic vinegar
4 tablespoons olive oil, divided
½ cup (100 ml) chopped parsley
1 bunch basil, chopped
sea salt flakes
freshly ground pepper
2 mozzarella balls
1 ripe mango

For Serving
¼ pound (100–150 g) Parma ham (Prosciutto di Parma)

1. Rinse the lentils and let drain. Divide the chili pepper lengthwise, remove the seeds and veins, and cut the halves into thin strips.

2. Blend together lentils, chili, garlic, tomatoes, balsamic vinegar, 2 tablespoons olive oil, and the herbs. Add salt and pepper to taste.

3. Cut the cheese into slices. Peel the mango, remove the flat seed, and cut the mango into slices.

4. Arrange the lentil salad on a plate and distribute cheese and mango over top. Drizzle the remainder of the olive oil over it, add salt and pepper to taste, and garnish with basil. Serve together with Parma ham.

Spinach Salad with Gnocchi and Rosemary Oil

These small balls made of cooked potatoes are perfect for a substantial salad. Toss them with a wonderful rosemary and garlic oil and they get a delightful flavor. Delicate spinach, pear, Pecorino Romano, and walnuts are all flavorful ingredients to add to the marinated gnocchi.

4 portions

2 tablespoons chopped fresh rosemary
2 garlic cloves, chopped
3 teaspoons sea salt flakes
⅓ cup (75 ml) olive oil
1 pound (500 g) gnocchi
2 ounces (50 g) baby spinach
2 pears
¾ cup (200 ml) coarsely grated Pecorino
    Romano or Parmesan
freshly ground pepper
2 ounces (50 g) walnuts

1. Crush rosemary, garlic, and salt in a mortar. Pour in the olive oil.

2. Cook the gnocchi according to the packaging directions. Drain. Toss the gnocchi with rosemary oil. Serve the gnocchi in the salad at room temperature or cold.

3. Rinse and dry the spinach. Cut the pears into wedges.

4. Carefully fold the gnocchi in with spinach, pears, and half of the cheese. Add salt and pepper to taste. Top with the rest of the cheese and nuts.

Pasta Salad Puttanesca with Salami

"A la puttanesca" means "a la whore" in Italian and is in actuality a rich tomato sauce with capers, anchovies, and olives. Here, I have made a pasta salad with the same salt and flavors.

4 portions

3 tablespoons olive oil
2 tablespoons freshly squeezed lemon juice
1 garlic clove, pressed
3 tablespoons thyme (with stems removed)
8 chopped anchovy fillets
10½ ounces (300 g) penne pasta
5 ounces (150 g) salami
1 package cherry-sized mozzarella balls
    (approx. 5 ounces/150 g)
9 ounces (250 g) cherry tomatoes
1 red onion
4 tablespoons capers
⅔ cup (150 ml) black olives
sea salt flakes
freshly ground black pepper
2 ounces (50 g) arugula

1. Mix together olive oil, lemon juice, garlic, thyme, and anchovies in a large bowl.

2. Cook the pasta according to the directions on the package. Let drain. Mix with the dressing.

3. Cut the salami into small cubes. Let the cheese drain. Halve the tomatoes and chop the onion.

4. Combine the pasta with salami, cheese, onion, capers, and olives. Add salt and pepper to taste.

5. Lastly, fold the tomatoes and the arugula into the salad.

Rhubarb Salad with Pepper Mackerel

You can certainly use rhubarb in a main course salad. I prefer to serve this healthy and fresh potato salad together with pepper mackerel, but it is good with all sorts of smoked or grilled fish.

4 portions

1¾ pounds (800 g) freshly cooked new potatoes
½ lemon, juice
3 tablespoons canola oil
1 tablespoon honey
sea salt flakes
freshly ground pepper
2 small fennel bulbs
½ pound (200 g) delicate rhubarb
½ cup (100 ml) chopped dill

For Serving
pepper mackerel

1. Cut the potatoes into smaller pieces. Combine lemon juice, oil, and honey. Fold in the potatoes and add salt and pepper to taste.

2. Slice the fennel bulbs as thinly as possible. Rinse and cut the rhubarb into strips.

3. Fold fennel, rhubarb, and dill into the salad just before serving. Serve the salad together with the mackerel.

Strawberry Tabbouleh with Lamb Loin au Gratin

Tabbouleh is a succulent Middle Eastern salad made of bulgur. In the summer, I prefer to toss strawberries into the salad. However, when berry season is over, I make the original recipe and substitute the strawberries for three deseeded and cubed tomatoes. The lamb loin au gratin with feta cheese and almond is a great accompaniment. The salad is also a home run with grilled lamb, spicy sausages, chicken, or pork shoulder—preferably together with the tzatziki on page 18.

4 portions

Meat
½ cup (100 ml) almonds
1 garlic clove, chopped
¾ cup (200 ml) coarsely
    chopped dill
¼ cup (50 ml) olive oil
3 ounces (100 g) goat cheese (chèvre)
sea salt flakes
freshly ground pepper
1–1¼ pounds (500–600 g) lamb loin
butter for frying

Tabbouleh
1 cup (250 ml) bulgur
2 cups (500 ml) vegetable broth
3 chopped shallots
½ cup (100 ml) coarsely chopped
    pistachios
¾ cup (200 ml) chopped parsley
½ cup (100 ml) chopped mint
3 tablespoons freshly squeezed lemon juice
3 tablespoons olive oil
sea salt flakes
freshly ground pepper
1¼–1¾ cup (300–400 ml) cut strawberries

1. **Begin with the Tabbouleh:** Boil the bulgur, covered, in the broth for about 10 minutes. Let the bulgur cool.

2. Combine bulgur, shallots, nuts, herbs, lemon juice, and olive oil. Add salt and pepper to taste.

3. Fold the strawberries into the salad just before serving.

4. **The Meat:** Mix together almond, garlic, dill, and olive oil. Crumble in the cheese and add salt and pepper to taste.

5. Preheat the oven to 425°F (225°C). Trim the loin free of sinews and fat. Brown on all sides in butter. Add salt and pepper to taste. Place the meat on a baking sheet lined with parchment paper. Stick a meat thermometer into the meat's thickest part.

6. Spread the topping over the meat. Roast in the middle of the oven until the thermometer shows 135°F (57°C) for pink meat. Remove from the oven and let it rest under aluminum foil for about 10 minutes. Slice the meat just before serving.

Summer Herring with Maître d' Potatoes

By tossing new potatoes with dill mustard sauce, we get a quick potato salad.
This is a perfect addition to the summer's soused herring or smoked fish.
I lay out the herring trimmings in different bowls so everyone can make
their own herring plate.

4 portions

2¼ pounds (1 kg) new potatoes
½ cup (100 ml) dill mustard sauce
½ cup (100 ml) chopped chives
¾ pound (400 g) soused herring fillets
⅔ cup (150 ml) chopped pickled beets
⅔ cup (150 ml) chopped apple
1 chopped red onion
½ cup (100 ml) capers

1. Scrub the potatoes clean. Boil in lightly salted water until tender.
Drain the remaining water and let the steam release.

2. Toss the potatoes with dill mustard sauce and chives.

3. Slice the herring into pieces. Arrange on a serving dish and garnish
with extra chives if needed.

4. Arrange the potato salad, beets, apple, onion, and capers in separate
bowls and serve with the herring.

Chickpea Salad with Halloumi

An exciting dressing made with sesame seeds, mint, and cilantro gives this salad an Oriental touch. Grilled halloumi and a spicy yogurt sauce strengthen the Oriental feeling. The salad and yogurt sauce are also good accompaniments to grilled lamb and spicy lamb sausages.

4 portions

4 tablespoons sesame seeds
2 garlic cloves, chopped
¾ cup (200 ml) fresh herbs: parsley, mint, cilantro
2 tablespoons freshly squeezed lemon juice
4 tablespoons olive oil
½ teaspoon Sambal Oelek
sea salt flakes
2 cans chickpeas (each 14 ounces/400 g)
3 ounces (100 g) dried apricots
1 red chili pepper
½ cup (100 ml) olives, preferably black and green
approx. 10½ ounces (300 g) halloumi
1 lemon
a couple of handfuls of arugula

Yogurt Sauce
1¾ cup (400 ml) Greek yogurt
2 garlic cloves, pressed
1 teaspoon ground cumin
sea salt flakes

1. Combine the ingredients for the yogurt sauce.

2. Roast the sesame seeds in a dry pan. Let cool. Mix sesame seeds, garlic, herbs, lemon juice, olive oil, Sambal Oelek, and salt.

3. Rinse the chickpeas and let drain. Mix the chickpeas with the sesame dressing.

4. Cut the apricots into thin strips. Split, remove seeds and chop the chili pepper. Mix chickpeas with apricots, chili, and olives.

5. Cut the halloumi into slices and fry in olive oil.

6. Serve the salad with freshly fried halloumi, lemon wedges, and yogurt sauce. Top with arugula.

Roasted Potato Salad with Roast Beef

Oven-roasted new potatoes taste glorious. This potato salad with gherkins, sun-dried cherry tomatoes, and capers is also a great dish for the summer barbecue. Homemade roast beef is, of course, the very best; however, it's sometimes necessary to take shortcuts in the kitchen. That's when store-bought roast beef is an excellent alternative. I usually get the roast beef cut extra thin, so that it feels juicier.

4 portions

2¼ pounds (1 kg) new potatoes
4 garlic cloves
2 + 2 tablespoons olive oil
1 lemon, zest and juice
2 tablespoons thyme (with stems removed)
sea salt flakes
freshly ground pepper
½ cup (100 ml) small gherkins
½ cup (100 ml) sun-dried cherry tomatoes in oil
3 tablespoons capers

For Serving
approx. ½ pound (200 g) extra thinly sliced roast beef

1. Preheat the oven to 400°F (200°C). Wash the potatoes and halve the larger ones. Place the potatoes and whole garlic cloves (with peel intact) on a baking sheet lined with parchment paper. Toss with 2 tablespoons olive oil.

2. Roast in the middle of the oven until the potatoes are tender, about 25 minutes. Stir occasionally.

3. Mash the roasted garlic cloves with the lemon zest and juice. Blend in 2 tablespoons olive oil, thyme, salt, and pepper.

4. Toss the potatoes with the dressing, gherkins, tomatoes, and capers. Add salt and pepper to taste. Serve with roast beef.

Farmer's Salad with Ham Hocks

When the thermometer dips into the negative numbers, you're probably not longing for a cold salad. Maybe this rustic salad with ham hocks, lentils, bacon, and croutons is just what you need.

4–6 portions

3⅓ pounds (1½ kg) ham hocks
1 carrot
1 yellow onion
½ tablespoon white peppercorns
5 whole allspice
2 bay leaves

Salad
5 ounces (140 g) bacon
1¼ cups (300 ml) croutons made of rustic bread
2 cans green lentils (each 14 ounces/400 g)
3 tablespoons coarsely ground mustard
¼ cup (50 ml) olive oil
1 tablespoon white wine vinegar
3 shallots, chopped
½ cup (100 ml) chopped parsley
sea salt flakes
freshly ground pepper
1 head frisée lettuce

1. **The Meat:** Place the meat in a thick-bottomed pot. Pour in enough water to cover the meat, and bring to a boil. Remove the meat and rinse under running water. Drain the excess water and wash out the pot.

2. Return the meat to the pot and pour in new water so that it is covered. Boil and skim the fat from the top. Peel the carrot and onion and slice into smaller pieces. Add the vegetables and spices to the pot.

3. Let the meat simmer over low heat, covered, for about 1½ hours. The meat is done when it starts to fall off the bone. Skim the fat from the broth while boiling so the broth is clear. Remove the pot from the heat and let the meat cool in its own broth. Remove the meat from the bone and divide into smaller pieces.

4. **The Salad:** Cut the bacon into fine strips and fry until crispy. Let it drain on paper towels. Bake the croutons in the oven at 425°F (225°C).

5. Rinse the lentils and let drain. Combine mustard, olive oil, and vinegar. Fold lentils, shallots, and parsley into the dressing. Add salt and pepper to taste.

6. Carefully combine the lettuce, lentils, and ham hocks. Top with croutons and bacon.

Autumn Salad with Pickled Mushrooms

In the fall, we have the opportunity to make use of what the forests and gardens have to offer. A warm and hearty salad made with root vegetables and mushrooms is both healthy and tasty to enjoy this time of the year.

4 portions

2 carrots
2 parsnips
1 rutabaga (approx. ¼ pound/150 g)
1 celeriac (approx. ¼ pound/150 g)
2 red onions
2 tablespoons olive oil
3 tablespoons fresh rosemary
sea salt flakes
10½ ounces (300 g) penne pasta
1¼–1¾ cups (300–400 ml) pickled mushrooms
2 tablespoons oil from the mushroom jar
1 tablespoon freshly squeezed lemon juice
freshly ground pepper
2 ounces (50 g) roasted pine nuts
approx. ¾ cup (200 ml) coarsely grated
    Parmesan cheese

1. Preheat the oven to 425°F (225°C) Peel the root vegetables and cut into smaller pieces. Peel and cut the onions into thick wedges. Place the root vegetables and onions on a baking sheet lined with parchment paper. Toss with olive oil, rosemary, and salt.

2. Roast the root vegetables in the middle of the oven about 25 minutes.

3. Meanwhile, boil the pasta according to the directions on the packaging. Let drain.

4. Combine root vegetables with freshly cooked pasta, mushrooms, oil, and lemon juice. Add salt and pepper to taste. Garnish with nuts and cheese.

Pickled Mushrooms in Olive Oil

Pickled mushrooms in olive oil are a wonderful way to preserve the autumn. Mushrooms are a good complement to wild game or Salisbury steak. You can also make them into a delicious little appetizer by laying the mushrooms on a garlic roasted crostini and grating Parmesan on top.

Approx. 4¼ cups

2¼ pounds (1 kg) fresh mushrooms
⅓ cup (75 ml) sea salt
1¼ cups (300 ml) white wine vinegar
6 black peppercorns
2 bay leaves
1¾–2 cups (400–500 ml) high quality olive oil

1. Rinse the mushrooms and slice into smaller pieces. Combine the mushrooms and salt in a large bowl and cover. Let absorb for about 12 hours at room temperature. Drain the liquid and dry the mushrooms on paper towels.

2. Boil the vinegar in a frying pan. Boil the mushrooms, covered, in two batches (half at a time) in the vinegar. Let them drain in a colander.

3. Move the mushrooms onto a tray lined with paper towels and let them drain for about two hours.

4. Place the mushrooms in a very clean 1 liter glass jar with a lid. Add the peppercorns and bay leaves. Pour in as much olive oil as needed to cover.

5. Close the lid and keep dark and cool. The mushrooms are ready to eat after 1–2 weeks, and can be stored for a couple of months in the fridge. Keep in mind that olive oil hardens in the refrigerator, so move the mushrooms to room temperature for a while before using.

Fruity Winter Salad with Duck Breast

Who said that winter food must be heavy and fatty? This Christmas-inspired winter salad is filled with goodies like stilton cheese, fresh figs, dates, kale, and walnuts.

4 portions

Duck Breast
2 duck breasts (each ⅔ pound/300 g)
sea salt flakes
freshly ground pepper
butter for frying

Salad
4 fresh figs
1 tablespoon butter
½ tablespoon raw sugar
4¼ cups (1 liter) thinly sliced kale, rinsed
1 endive
2 clementines, in wedges
½ red onion, sliced
approx. 5 ounces (150 g) stilton or other bleu cheese
½ cup (100 ml) fresh dates, in pieces
2 ounces (50 g) walnuts
2 tablespoons aged balsamic vinegar or crema di balsamico
¼ cup (50 ml) hazelnut oil
sea salt flakes
freshly ground pepper

1. **The Duck Breast:** Slice a pattern into the fatty side of the duck breast and add salt and pepper to taste.

2. Heat a frying pan over high heat and add butter. Reduce the temperature and place the duck breast in the pan, patterned side down, and fry for 5 minutes. Flip and continue to fry for about 3 minutes. The duck breast should be pink inside.

3. Wrap the duck breast in aluminum foil and let rest about 5 minutes. Cut into thin slices just before serving.

4. **The Salad:** Split the figs down the middle and fry the cut side in butter together with the sugar until tender.

5. Arrange the kale, endive leaves, clementines, onion, crumbled cheese, dates, figs, and split nuts on plates. Drizzle with vinegar and oil and add salt and pepper to taste.

Chicken Salad with Pasta and Bleu Cheese

Warm salad is a wonderfully inviting food! Right before serving, combine the warm ingredients with the remaining ingredients and serve on a generous platter. This salad works well for barbeque season, as the chicken thigh is terrific for grilling. It will cook quickly without drying out. And when you are still in a grilling mood, substitute the bleu cheese with halloumi, and grill slices.

4 portions

¾ pound (400 g) beets
3⅓ cups (800 ml) loosely
    packed baby spinach
4 tablespoons pine nuts
7 ounces (200 g) penne pasta
1 pound (500 g) boneless chicken
    thigh fillets
olive oil for frying
sea salt flakes
freshly ground black pepper
approx. 5 ounces (150 g) bleu cheese

Dressing
3 tablespoons olive oil
2 tablespoons aged balsamic vinegar or
    crema di balsamico
sea salt flakes
freshly ground pepper

1. Begin by combining the ingredients for the dressing.

2. Boil the beets in lightly salted water until tender. The amount of time required depends on the size of the beets. Let the root ends and a little stem remain when boiling them, as this retains the color and they taste better.

3. Rinse the beets quickly under cold running water and pull away the skins while they are warm. Slice the beets into wedges and preferably keep them warm.

4. Rinse and drain the spinach. Roast the pine nuts in a dry pan. Cook the pasta, drain the excess water, and blend with a little olive oil.

5. Fry the chicken thigh fillets in olive oil for about 3 minutes. Add salt and pepper to taste. Keep the chicken warm under foil. Cut into slices just before serving.

6. Combine the beets, pasta, spinach, chicken, and crumbled cheese. Drizzle with dressing and garnish with nuts.

Kippers Niçoise

A successful combination of Provence and the Nordic countries, salad Niçoise with kippers and dill is really a delightful summer salad. I truly believe that this classic salad tastes more exciting with kippers than with the original tuna.

4 portions

4–6 potatoes
½ pound (250 g) haricots verts (or green beans)
½ pound (250 g) cherry tomatoes
1 red onion
3 tablespoons chopped dill
4 tablespoons olive oil
1 lemon, juice
sea salt flakes
freshly ground pepper
½ cup (100 ml) black olives
2 tablespoons capers
2 hardboiled eggs

For Serving
kippers

1. Brush the potatoes clean and boil in lightly salted water. Let cool and cut into pieces.

2. Boil the beans in lightly salted water. Halve the tomatoes and slice the onion thinly.

3. Toss together potatoes, beans, tomatoes, onion, dill, oil, and lemon juice. Add salt and pepper to taste.

4. Arrange the salad and distribute olives, capers, and egg wedges on top. Serve the salad together with the kippers.

Orzo with Smoked Salmon and Saffron

A pasta salad with smoked salmon, saffron, and vegetables is perfect to take with you in the picnic basket. Orzo looks like rice but is actually a type of pasta.

4 portions

1 yellow onion
olive oil
a pinch (½ g) of saffron
3⅓ cups (800 ml) water
2 vegetable bouillon cubes
1¾ cups (400 ml) orzo
¾ cup (200 ml) green peas
½–⅔ pound (250–300 g) smoked salmon, warm
approx. ½ pound (200 g) cherry tomatoes
1 small red pepper
3½ ounces (100 g) baby spinach
sea salt flakes
freshly ground pepper
lemon wedges for garnish

1. Chop the onion and fry in olive oil a few minutes without letting it change color. Toward the end, add the saffron.

2. Add the water, bouillon, and orzo and boil gently, covered, for about 11 minutes. Add in the peas when a few minutes of cooking time remain. Let the orzo cool.

3. Cut the salmon into smaller pieces. Halve the tomatoes and cut the pepper into small cubes.

4. Carefully fold the salmon, tomatoes, pepper, and spinach into the salad. Add salt and pepper to taste and garnish with lemon wedges.

Nectarine Salad with Pepper Steak

Most people appreciate good meat. Forget the gravy and invite everyone over for the summer's freshest salad instead. All too often, the nectarines we find in grocery stores are too firm to eat. However, when they are hard, they are not that sweet and are exceptional in a main course salad.

4 portions

Pepper Steak
approx. 1¼ pounds (600 g) trimmed beef, cut into pieces
1½ teaspoons coarsely crushed black peppercorns
1½ teaspoons coarsely crushed pink peppercorns
sea salt flakes
butter for frying

Salad
4 nectarines
3½ ounces (100 g) sugar snap peas
4 green onions
3 tablespoons freshly squeezed lemon juice
¼ cup (50 ml) olive oil
sea salt flakes
freshly ground pepper
approx. 1¾ cup (400 ml) watercress

1. **The Meat:** Divide the meat in slices approximately 1½ inches thick. Rub the slices of meat with the crushed peppers.

2. Fry the meat 2 to 3 minutes per side on medium high heat. The frying time depends on how rare you like your meat cooked. Flip the meat carefully so the peppercorns remain in place. Add salt to taste.

3. Place the meat onto a cutting board and cover with aluminum foil. Let rest about 5 minutes. Cut the meat diagonally into fairly thin slices and serve together with the salad.

4. **The Salad:** Halve the nectarines and remove the seeds. Cut them into wedges as thin as possible. Cut the sugar snap peas and onions into thin strips.

5. Stir together lemon juice, olive oil, salt, and pepper. Combine with nectarines, sugar snap peas, and onions. Fold the watercress into the salad just before serving.

Beet Quinoa with Chicken

A juicy, fresh, healthy, and beautiful red chicken salad. What more can you ask for?

4 portions

approx. ¾ pound (400 g) beets
¾ cup (200 ml) quinoa
2 cups (500 ml) chicken broth
¾ pound (400 g) boneless chicken thigh fillets
butter
sea salt flakes
freshly ground pepper
10½ ounces (300 g) goat cheese (chèvre)
9 ounces (250 g) quark or cottage cheese
2 tablespoons olive oil
1 tablespoon freshly squeezed lemon juice
1 red onion, sliced
2 ounces (50 g) arugula
3 ounces (75 g) walnuts

1. Peel the beets and cut into ½ inch pieces. Boil the quinoa and beets in the broth, about 15 minutes. Drain and let the steam release.

2. Fry the chicken in butter. Add salt and pepper to taste. Keep warm under foil.

3. Crumble the goat cheese. Combine half of the cheese with the quark or cottage cheese.

4. Combine the quinoa, olive oil, lemon juice, onion, arugula, and nuts. Add salt and pepper to taste.

5. Top with chicken and crumble the rest of the goat cheese on top. Serve the salad with the goat cheese cream.

Melon Salad with Feta Cheese and Black Beans

Watermelon and feta cheese are unbelievably tasty on a warm summer day. With beans, this becomes a substantial lunch salad.

4 portions

1 can black beans (approx. 14 ounces/400 g)
1 red onion
5 ounces (150 g) sugar snap peas
3 tablespoons pumpkin seeds
¼ cup (50 ml) olive oil
1 lime, juice
1 tablespoon honey
sea salt flakes
freshly ground pepper
1¼ pounds (500 g) cubed watermelon
2 tablespoons chopped fresh mint
7 ounces (200 g) feta cheese

1. Rinse the beans and let drain. Peel and slice the onion. Cut the sugar snap peas into thin strips.

2. Roast the pumpkin seeds in a dry pan.

3. Combine oil, lime juice, honey, salt, and pepper in a large bowl.

4. Fold the beans, onion, sugar snap peas, melon, and mint into the dressing just before serving.

5. Arrange the salad and garnish with crumbled cheese and pumpkin seeds.

Marinated Tuna and Pasta Salad

Marinated tuna is really practical to bring with you on picnics in the countryside or on the boat. In the summer I usually serve the tuna with this pasta salad, and in the winter I mix it with freshly cooked pasta. Try spreading the tuna onto a slice of toasted country bread—yummy! Consider using whole tuna fillets of high quality. If there is any olive oil left over from the marinade, it's tasty to drizzle over fish and shellfish salads.

4–6 portions

Marinated Tuna
2 cans tuna fish in oil (whole fillet)
⅓ cup (75 ml) thinly sliced sun-dried tomatoes
¼ cup (50 ml) capers
½ cup (100 ml) black olives
½ bunch thyme
1¼–1¾ cups (300–400 ml) high quality olive oil

Pasta Salad
10½ ounces (300 g) penne
4 tablespoons olive oil from the tuna fish
2 tablespoons freshly squeezed lemon juice
1 red onion, chopped
½ pound (250 g) cherry tomatoes
approx. 2 ounces (50 g) baby spinach or arugula
sea salt flakes
freshly ground pepper
½ bunch basil

1. **The Tuna:** Let the tuna drain. Alternate layers of tuna, tomatoes, capers, olives, and thyme sprigs in a jar. Pour in enough olive oil to cover the tuna, and close the lid.

2. Let the tuna marinate a few days before serving. Store in the fridge, but leave it at room temperature for an adequate amount of time before serving.

3. **The Salad:** Cook the pasta according to the directions on the packaging. Let drain and mix in the oil.

4. Mix in the lemon juice, onion, halved tomatoes, and spinach or arugula. Add salt and pepper to taste.

5. Arrange the salad and distribute the marinated tuna over top. Garnish with basil.

Eggplant Caviar with Melon and Ham

Eggplant spreads are found in every Mediterranean country but the flavors may vary. In the Middle East, eggplants are grilled to give the spread a smoky flavor. Here I've made a milder variant from southern France that is called eggplant caviar and is very tasty with ham and sweet melon.

4 portions

Melon Plate
1 small melon such as ogen melon or cantaloupe
approx. ¼ pound (150 g) Parma ham (Prosciutto di Parma)
½ bunch basil
baguette

Eggplant Caviar
3 eggplants
1 tablespoon tomato purée
1 tablespoon freshly squeezed lemon juice
2 garlic cloves, chopped
½ cup (100 ml) olive oil
sea salt flakes
freshly ground pepper

1. **The Eggplant Caviar:** Preheat the oven to 350°F (175°C). Halve the eggplants lengthwise and score them lightly across the surface. Lay them on the oven rack with the cut side facing up.

2. Bake the eggplant in the middle of the oven for about one hour. Let the eggplant cool a bit and scoop out the eggplant flesh.

3. Mix the eggplant, tomato puree, lemon juice, and garlic. Stir in the olive oil and add salt and pepper to taste.

4. **The Melon Plate:** Cut the melon into wedges and scrape out the seeds. Arrange the melon and ham and garnish with basil. Serve together with eggplant caviar and bread.

Warm Bean and Chicken Salad

Quick, tasty, and healthy food is the epitome of everyday luxury. It's wonderful that there are so many different canned beans, and each makes a really good base for a hearty salad. Fruit and chicken are always tasty together, and the beans and avocado make this meal more filling.

4 portions

¾ pound (400 g) chicken breast
olive oil for frying
2 teaspoons rosemary
sea salt flakes
freshly ground pepper
2 grapefruits
2 cans borlotti beans (each 14 ounces/400 g)
2 avocadoes
1 red onion
approx. 1 ounce (25 g) arugula
2 tablespoons freshly squeezed grapefruit juice
3 tablespoons olive oil

1. Cut the chicken into smaller pieces. Fry for a few minutes in olive oil and the rosemary. Add salt and pepper to taste.

2. Peel the grapefruits with a knife until the white part is completely removed. Cut out the skinless wedges between the membranes of the grapefruit. Squeeze the juice from the membranes.

3. Rinse the beans and let drain. Peel the avocado and cut into slices. Peel and slice the onion.

4. Carefully combine the beans, grapefruit wedges, and vegetables with arugula, grapefruit juice, and oil. Add salt and pepper to taste. Distribute the chicken over the salad.

Dips and Spreads

Various spreads and dips are an exceptional addition for salads—and other dishes too, for that matter. That they're simple and quick to mix or blend together is an added bonus. Remember to let the spreads and dips sit for a while, preferably for a few hours, so the flavor has time to develop.

Carrot Pesto
approx. 1¾ cups (400 ml)

7 ounces (200 g) boiled carrots
2 ounces (50 g) walnuts
1 garlic clove, chopped
⅔ cup (150 ml) grated cheddar or other strong cheese
1 tablespoon freshly squeezed lemon juice
⅔ cup (150 ml) canola oil
sea salt flakes
freshly ground pepper

Blend the ingredients. Add salt and pepper to taste.

Spicy Yogurt Dip
approx. 1¼ cups (300 ml)

1¼ cups (300 ml) Greek yogurt
1 tablespoon olive oil
1 garlic clove, pressed
½ lemon, zest
½ chili pepper,
chopped
2 tablespoons chopped dill
1 tablespoon chopped mint
sea salt flakes

Combine all ingredients and add salt to taste.

Feta Dip
approx. 2 cups (500 ml)

4 red peppers
2 ounces (50 g) pine nuts
1 garlic clove, pressed
¼ cup (50 ml) olive oil
5 ounces (150 g) feta cheese
sea salt flakes
freshly ground pepper

1. Preheat the oven to 475°F (250°C). Split the peppers into four pieces and remove the seeds and pith. Grill them on the top rack of the oven with the cupped side up until the skin is black and bruised, about 20 minutes.

2. Place the peppers into a plastic bag for about 10 minutes so it is easier to remove the skin. Remove the skin.

3. Mix together peppers, nuts, garlic, and olive oil.

4. Add in crumbled cheese. Add salt and pepper to taste.

Cheddar Cream
approx. 2 cups (500 ml)

3½ ounces (100 g) cream cheese
9 ounces (250 g) quark or cottage cheese
⅔ cup coarsely grated cheddar cheese
¼ cup (50 ml) celery, cut into fine strips
3 tablespoons chopped red onion
1 ounce (25 g) chopped walnuts
¼ cup chopped parsley
sea salt flakes
freshly ground pepper

1. Stir together cream cheese and quark or cottage cheese.

2. Blend in cheddar, celery, onion, nuts, and parsley. Add salt and pepper to taste.

Arugula Dip
approx. 1¾ cups (400 ml)

1 ounce (25 g) arugula
3½ ounces (100 g) cream cheese
¾ cup (200 ml) light crème fraîche or sour cream
1 garlic clove, pressed
½ cup (100 ml) grated Parmesan cheese
sea salt flakes
freshly ground pepper

1. Chop the arugula. Combine the arugula, cream cheese, and crème fraîche.

2. Add in the garlic and Parmesan. Add salt and pepper to taste.

Red Lentil Hummus
approx. 1¾ cups (400 ml)

¾ cup (200 ml) red lentils
3 tablespoons olive oil
1 tablespoon freshly squeezed lemon juice
1 garlic clove, pressed
1 teaspoon paprika
½ teaspoon ground cumin
1 red chili pepper, chopped
sea salt flakes
freshly ground pepper

1. Boil the lentils according to the instructions on the packaging, about 10 minutes. Let drain in a colander.

2. Combine lentils, olive oil, lemon juice, garlic, paprika, and cumin. Add in the chili pepper. Add salt and pepper to taste.

Green Basil Tapenade
approx. 1¾ cups (400 ml)

1¼ cups (300 ml) green pitted olives
4 garlic cloves, chopped
3 tablespoons chopped basil
6 anchovies
3 tablespoons capers
½ lemon, juice
½ cup (100 ml) olive oil
freshly ground pepper

1. Blend all ingredients together, except olive oil and pepper, for a coarse consistency.

2. Pour in olive oil and add pepper to taste.

Chèvre Cream
approx. 1¾ cups (400 ml)

7 ounces (200 g) chèvre (goat cheese)
9 ounces (250 g) quark or cottage cheese
¼ cup (50 ml) chopped sun-dried tomatoes in oil
¼ cup (50 ml) chopped black olives
1 tablespoon chopped capers
½ bunch basil
sea salt flakes
freshly ground pepper

1. Combine the chèvre with the quark or cottage cheese until you get a smooth cream.

2. Add in tomatoes, olives, capers, and basil. Add salt and pepper to taste.

Artichoke Dip

approx. 1¾ cups (400 ml)

1 can artichoke hearts (approx. 14 ounces/400 g)
⅓ cup (75 ml) pine nuts
1 garlic clove, chopped
1 bunch of basil
½ lemon, juice
1½ cups (350 ml) olive oil
½ cup (100 ml) freshly grated Parmesan cheese
sea salt flakes
freshly ground pepper

1. Drain the artichoke hearts.

2. Blend artichoke hearts, nuts, garlic, and basil. Mix in lemon juice, olive oil, and Parmesan. Add salt and pepper to taste.

Mojo

approx. 1¾ cups

1 can roasted red peppers in oil
    (approx. 7 ounces/200 g)
approx. ¼ cup (50 ml) olive oil
1 garlic clove, chopped
1 slice white bread with crusts removed
1 tablespoon red wine vinegar
1 teaspoon honey
sea salt flakes

1. Let the peppers drain, but save the oil. Add olive oil to the oil from the red peppers until you get a ½ cup.

2. Blend peppers, garlic, bread, vinegar, and honey to an even mixture.

3. Pour in the oil, a little at a time, so that the combination doesn't separate. Add salt to taste.

Bean Dip with Lemon and Mint

approx. 1¾ cups (400 ml)

1 can cannellini beans (approx. 14 ounces/400 g)
1 garlic clove, chopped
¼ cup (50 ml) quark or cottage cheese
½ lemon, zest and juice
1 tablespoon chopped mint
¼ cup (50 ml) olive oil
sea salt flakes
freshly ground pepper

1. Rinse the beans and let drain.

2. Blend together the ingredients and add salt and pepper to taste.

Herb Cream Cheese

approx. 1¾ cups (400 ml)

3½ ounces (100 g) cream cheese, room temperature
9 ounces (250 g) quark or cottage cheese
1 garlic clove, pressed
½ cup (100 ml) coarsely grated Parmesan cheese
1 bunch basil, finely chopped
¼ cup (50 ml) chopped parsley
sea salt flakes
freshly ground pepper

1. Combine together cream cheese and quark or cottage cheese.

2. Add in garlic, Parmesan, and herbs, and add salt and pepper to taste.

Dressings

Often the dressing is the "cherry on top" of the salad. And seeing that they are so simple to stir together and also have a good shelf life, you can always keep different types on hand in the fridge.

Olive and Caper Vinaigrette 4 portions

2 teaspoons white wine vinegar
½ cup (100 ml) olive oil
2 chopped anchovies
2 tablespoons coarsely chopped black olives
1 garlic clove, pressed
2 teaspoons chopped capers
2 tablespoons basil
freshly ground pepper

Pour the vinegar into a bowl. Whisk in the oil, a little at a time. Combine in the rest of the ingredients and add pepper to taste.

Summer Sauce 4 portions

1¼ cups (300 ml) sour cream
¼ cup (50 ml) mayonnaise
1½ tablespoons spicy brown mustard
1 small finely chopped red onion
½ teaspoon Italian seasoning
½ cup (100 ml) chopped chives
¼ cup (50 ml) chopped dill
sea salt flakes
freshly ground pepper

Combine the ingredients for the dressing and add salt and pepper to taste. Let the flavors develop for about 1 hour before serving.

Herb Garden Dressing 4 portions

1¼ cups (300 ml) crème fraîche or sour cream
3 tablespoons mayonnaise
½ cup (100 ml) chopped fresh herbs such as basil, parsley, dill, chives, tarragon
1 garlic clove
1 teaspoon lemon pepper
sea salt flakes

Combine all ingredients and add salt to taste. Let the flavors develop approximately one hour before serving.

Tomato Vinaigrette 4 portions

4 sun-dried tomatoes in oil
1 teaspoon chopped fresh rosemary
1 garlic clove
1 teaspoon red wine vinegar
¼ teaspoon sugar
½ cup (100 ml) olive oil
sea salt flakes
freshly ground pepper

Finely chop the tomatoes. Mix the ingredients with an immersion blender. Add salt and pepper to taste.

French Mustard Dressing 4 portions

1 egg yolk
2 tablespoons Dijon mustard
¾ cup (200 ml) canola oil
sea salt flakes
freshly ground white pepper

Combine the egg yolk and mustard. Whisk in the oil with an electric mixer, a little at a time, so that the dressing doesn't separate. Add salt and pepper to taste. Dilute with a little water if it is too thick.

Red Onion Vinaigrette 4 portions

2 teaspoons red wine vinegar
½ teaspoon sugar
½ cup (100 ml) canola oil
3 tablespoons finely chopped red onion
2 tablespoons chopped parsley
sea salt flakes
freshly ground pepper

Combine the vinegar and sugar. Whisk in the oil, a little at a time. Blend in the onion and parsley and add salt and pepper to taste.

Salad Bases

Different seeds and herbs make hearty salad bases and add a pleasant variety. All whole grain products should be cooked without salt, otherwise they can close up instead of splitting open. Cook as directed with water. Pick up a grain and taste it to test if it is soft all over. Drain the excess water. If you would like to salt it, or add flavor with bouillon, do so at the end of the cooking time, or when the grain is fully cooked. Cooking time can vary, so always read the instructions on the packaging.

Couscous

Couscous originally comes from Northern Africa. Couscous is actually not a grain, but is a hard dough that is pressed through increasingly finer sieves. Then it gets dried. Originally, this was a method of conserving the wheat. Seeing that neither bran nor germ is included, the couscous becomes poorer in both fiber and nutrients than bulgur. There is also whole grain couscous which, in terms of fiber, lies right between regular couscous and bulgur.

Cooking time: about 5 minutes

Spelt

Spelt, or dinkel, is an ancient type of wheat that originates from the early wheat such as emmer wheat and wild goat-grass. Spelt began to develop in Sweden in the Stone Age, but from the Viking era, other easier-to-care-for seed types that give larger yields became more popular. Spelt is not refined in the same way as normal wheat, and we usually say it has its own original characteristics left. Some of these give a better flavor and a better nutritional content. It's important to remember that spelt contains just as much gluten as normal wheat, but some people with a sensitive stomach say they feel better from spelt than from regular wheat.

Cooking time for whole wheat: about 40 minutes

Bulgur

Bulgur was likely the first product refined out of wheat before the millstone was invented. This had the power to grind wheat into flour. Bulgur is rich in proteins, fiber, minerals, and vitamins since it contains the whole wheat grain. You get bulgur through first cooking and then drying whole durum wheat. Bulgur has definitely come to stay and is an excellent addition to salads and a good alternative to rice, potatoes, and pasta.

Cooking time: about 10 minutes

Buckwheat

Buckwheat is an herb that has long been popular in health circles. It is used as a cereal, but is still free from gluten and therefore a good alternative for the gluten-intolerant. Buckwheat has good protein quality and is rich in minerals. Some people might dislike the red coloring in buckwheat. To remove the coloring, you should either pour boiling water over the buckwheat before cooking or pour out the water that the buckwheat is boiled in and fill with new cooking water. Buckwheat has a low glycemic index and tends to be gentle on the stomach. When buckwheat is eaten like rice or in a salad, it's good to first roast it in a pot until it is dry. On the one hand, because it gives a good flavor, and the other, you get drier buckwheat that doesn't stick together so much. Otherwise buckwheat gets slimy when wet, which makes it into a perfect binding agent for ground meat.

Cooking time for whole buckwheat: about 10 minutes

Quinoa

Quinoa is actually an herb, but it is used as a type of seed. The most common thing is to use quinoa instead of rice, but during the last few years quinoa has also become a popular salad base. Quinoa is unusually protein rich and the protein contained is of a high quality. Aside from vitamins and minerals, quinoa has a fairly high fat percentage at around 5 percent. Quinoa doesn't contain gluten and is easy to digest, even for sensitive stomachs. Always rinse quinoa in hot water before cooking to remove the bitter taste.

Cooking time: about 15 minutes

Kamut wheat: The original wheat

Kamut is unrefined wheat and has a seed double the size of regular wheat. The original came from the Nile Delta. It is said that kamut seeds were found in the pyramids of Egypt, but they were probably purchased by a merchant who visited the country in 1949. The seeds ended up in the United States and kamut began to germinate there, but it wasn't before the end of the 1980s that germination seriously began. Kamut wheat has a higher percentage of minerals, proteins, and vitamins than regular wheat and a tasty, nutty flavor.

Cooking time for whole grain: 40 minutes

Whole Oat Groats

Whole oat groats are an old seed type that is beginning to become popular once again. Whole oat groats are a type of oat, though without the hull. It has more flavor and contains better nutrients than regular oats. They're called "naked" oats because the husk falls off when it's threshed. Whole oat groats can be bought in both grain and whole grain. The grain is used for oatmeal and the whole grain is exceptionally suited to eat like rice, or to add into salads.

Cooking time for whole grain: 25–30 minutes

Barley

Barley belongs to the oldest cereal species. Once upon a time it was an essential foodstuff. Lately, it seems that barley has seen a surge in popularity, likely due to all the other grains that have been rediscovered. The normal type in stores is husked and cut barley. The cooking time varies depending on how much of the grain is intact. In salads, it is important to use whole barley as the crushed has a tendency to turn into gruel. If you don't find whole barley, for consistency's sake it is better to use pearl barley. Pearl barley is steam processed barley that is cut into pieces and has a cooking time of approximately 8 minutes. Barley has an unusually low glycemic index.

Cooking time for whole barley: about 50 minutes

Recipe Index

Lamb kebab, halloumi potatoes with 95
Lamb loin au gratin, strawberry tabbouleh with 140
Lamb, rack of, minty beans with 63
Lamb tenderloin, Thai salad with 133
Lentil salad with mozzarella and mango 134
Lime yogurt 45
Lingonberries, bulgur wheat with chanterelles and, 9
Lingonberry and red cabbage salad with black pudding 121

Mango and sesame salmon, glass noodle salad with 78
Marinated tuna and pasta salad 174
Melon and ham with chive-tossed potatoes 115
Melon and ham, eggplant caviar with 177
Melon and egg hummus, smoked salmon with 109
Melon salad with feta cheese and black beans 173
Mezze platter 124
Minty beans with rack of lamb 63
Mojo 185
Mortadella, pesto beans with 16
Mozzarella and mango, lentil salad with 134
Mozzarella, grilled asparagus with 21
Mozzarella toast, tomato salad with 70
Mushroom couscous with venison and sharp cheddar cream 32
Mushrooms, pickled, in olive oil, 155
Mushrooms, pickled, autumn salad with 155
Mushroom salad, roasted, with bacon 80
Mussels, smoked, and bacon, creamy lentils with 96

Nectarine salad with pepper steak 166
New potato Caesar with crayfish and Prästost cheese 66
New potatoes, Greek salad with 37

Olive oil, pickled mushrooms in 155
Oriental bulgur with halloumi 127
Orzo with smoked salmon and saffron 165

Parsnip salad with hazelnut vinaigrette 80
Pasta and bleu cheese, chicken salad with 161
Pasta salad, marinated tuna and 174
Pasta salad puttanesca with salami 137
Pear salad, toast au chèvre chaud with 100
Pepper mackerel, rhubarb salad with 139
Pepper steak, nectarine salad with 166
Pepper strawberries with goat cheese chicken 106
Pesto beans with mortadella 16
Pickled herring salad with beets and browned butter 52
Pickled mushrooms in olive oil 155
Poached salmon, creamy potato salad with 123
Pork belly, barley salad with roasted beets and 93
Pork tenderloin with warm feta cheese salad 90
Potato salad with smoked salmon and shrimp 118

Quinoa salad with peaches, goat cheese, and Parma ham 74

Red cabbage salad with chicken kebab 77
Red lentil hummus 184
Red onion vinaigrette 186
Rhubarb salad with pepper mackerel 139
Rib eye, grilled, sautéed broccoli with 60
Roasted asparagus with bacon 21
Roasted mushroom salad with bacon 80
Roast beef and bean salad with coarse tapenade 34
Roast beef, roasted potato salad with 148
Root vegetable omelet with brie and kale salad 69
Root vegetable salad with spelt and venison dip 55
Root vegetable salad with spelt berries and kale pesto 128
Rosemary-fried chicken liver with bean salad 51

Salad tartar, beef Tenderloin with 27
Salad with peaches and ham toast au gratin 100
Salami, pasta salad puttanesca with 137
Salmon bulgur with lime yogurt 45
Sautéed broccoli with grilled rib eye 60
Shrimp salad with Thousand Island dressing 23
Smoked salmon and saffron, orzo with 165
Smoked salmon and shrimp, potato salad with 118
Smoked salmon with melon and egg hummus 109

Spicy sausage with warm beet salad 112
Spicy yogurt dip 183
Spinach salad with gnocchi and rosemary oil 137
Spelt and venison dip, root vegetable salad with 55
Spring vegetable salad with smoked fish and egg 83
Spring vegetable salad with smoked turkey breast 28
Strawberry tabbouleh with lamb loin au gratin 140
Summer herring with maître d' potatoes 145
Summer sauce 186

Thai salad with lamb tenderloin 133
Thousand Island dressing, shrimp salad with 23
Toast au chèvre chaud with pear salad 100
Tomato couscous with feta 32
Tomato salad with mozzarella toast 70
Tomato vinaigrette 186
Tuna sauce, chicken salad with 12
Turkey, cauliflower with bleu cheese and 111
Turkey breast, smoked, spring vegetable salad with 28
Turkey, warm apple salad with 47
Tzatziki, bulgur-stuffed eggplant with 18

Warm apple salad with turkey 47
Warm bean and chicken salad 178
Warm fennel salad with oven-baked salmon 89
Warm pasta salad with bleu cheese 48
Warm root vegetable salad with ham and gorgonzola cream 31
Warm salad with tortellini and arugula dressing 73